HANDBOOK OF BUDGET
Third Edition

HANDBOOK OF BUDGETING
Third Edition

1994 Supplement

Robert Rachlin
H.W. Allen Sweeny

JOHN WILEY & SONS, INC.

New York   •   Chichester   •   Brisbane   •   Toronto   •   Singapore

Library of Congress Cataloging in Publication Data

Handbook of budgeting / [edited by] Robert Rachlin, H.W. Allen
  Sweeny,—3rd. ed.
      p.   cm.
  Includes bibliographical references and index.
  ISBN 0-471-57771-5 (cloth)
  ISBN 0-471-05836-X (supplement)
  1. Budget in business. I. Rachlin, Robert, 1937–
II. Sweeny, Allen.
  HG4028.B8H36 1993
  658.15′4—dc20   92-39299

ABOUT THE AUTHORS

Robert Rachlin, President of Robert Rachlin Associates, is an internationally known author, lecturer, and consultant in the area of financial management and serves as Assistant Dean for Business Studies, Hofstra University. He has previously served as vice president of several companies in planning and budgeting capacities. Mr. Rachlin received a BBA in accounting from Pace University and an MBA in management and economics from St. John's University. He has also served as an Adjunct Associate Professor of Management at New York University, and the New York Institute of Technology. He is currently an Adjunct Professor of Management at Hofstra University. Mr. Rachlin is a frequent lecturer to professional groups, companies, and practicing professionals, and is the recipient of the "Fellow" Award for outstanding service to the planning profession by the Planning Executives Institute, an organization for which he served as New York Chapter President. He is also the author and/or co-editor of *Successful Techniques for Higher Profits, Return on Investment-Strategies for Decision-Making, Handbook of Strategic Planning, Total Business Budgeting: A Step-by-Step Guide with Forms,* and *Managing Cash Flow and Capital During Inflation.*

H.W. Allen Sweeny retired as Senior Vice President and Chief Financial Officer of Del Monte Foods when that multi-billion-dollar international food company closed its world headquarters in Miami in 1990. Prior to that he served in a variety of financial development and general management positions for R.J.R. Nabisco and Exxon while living in Argentina, Colombia, Hong Kong, Japan, and the United States. Mr. Sweeny has a BS in General Business from the University of Kansas and an MBA from the Harvard Graduate School of Business Administration. He has authored and/or edited six books on accounting, budgeting, strategic planning, and financial management and has lectured and taught these subjects at the Fordham Graduate School of Business.

PREFACE

The 1994 supplement contains three new chapters. Chapter 11A, "Budgeting Shareholder Value," describes how shareholders provide an economic measurement of business performance. Shareholder value is used to increase future growth as measured by the sum of future cash flows in today's dollars. The chapter presents a detailed analysis of how to budget and calculate and reasons why shareholder value must be part of today's budgeting process.

Chapter 20A, "Leasing," explores the leasing process and how the operating budget is affected. This chapter includes such topics as lease reporting, FASB 13 case illustrations, and lease analysis techniques.

Chapter 27A, "Activity-Based Budgeting," presents a complete detailed study on the activity-based budgeting process, from linking strategy and budgeting to translating strategies to activities; from determining workloads to creating planning guidelines; from finalizing the budget to performance reporting. This is a state-of-the-art look at the ABB process.

In addition to the three new chapters, minor updates were made in three chapters and a major revision to chapter 15.

Plainview, New York

ROBERT RACHLIN
Chief Editor

Miami, Florida
May 1994

H.W. ALLEN SWEENY
Coeditor

CONTRIBUTORS

Page ix, add after entry for James W. Anderson:

John Antos is a management consultant specializing in activity-based management, quality costs, acquisitions, planning, and modern cost systems. He consults and lectures around the world to major companies and is a recognized professional in his field. He has been a chief financial officer, director, and controller within industry and has turned around a company on the verge of bankruptcy. He has consulted on such topics as ABM, ABC, ABB, accounting systems, strategic planning, plant expansion studies, acquisitions, and marketing. Mr. Antos has an MBA in Accounting and Marketing from the University of Chicago and his BS in Business Administration from the University of Illinois-Urbana. He is also a Certified Management Accountant and a Certified Financial Planner.

Robert D. Apgood, PhD, is a leasing and financial consultant specializing in international leasing, accounting, and finance. He is a CPA and has an MBA and a PhD in accounting. Dr. Apgood has served as chairman of the Accounting Standards Committee for the broadcast industry, as vice president of finance for a broadcasting and telecommunications conglomerate, and as a full professor of accounting. In addition to his consulting practice, he is currently vice president of a high-tech bioremediation firm.

James A. Brimson is President of Activity Based Management—Institute, an international confederation of consulting, training, and software companies who specialize in activity-based management. Prior to ABM-I, Mr. Brimson served as partner-in-charge of Coopers & Lybrand, Deloitte's worldwide activity-based management consulting practice in London, England. He also served as director of CAM-I (an international consortium) with more than 13 years of industry experience concentrating in cost management and systems development activities, primarily in the manufacturing industry. Mr. Brimson is the author of *Activity Accounting—An Activity-Based Costing Approach,* published by John Wiley & Sons, Inc., and coeditor of *Cost Management for Today's Advanced Manufacturing, The CAM-I Conceptual Design,* published by Harvard Business School Press. He has a BS from Auburn University and an MBA in quantitative science from Arizona State University.

page xi, replace entry for Eugene H. Kramer with:

Eugene H. Kramer, CPA, deceased, was a principal in the firm of E.H. Kramer and Company.

Page xii, replace entry for R. Malcolm Schwartz with:

R. Malcolm Schwartz is a partner with Coopers & Lybrand and is responsible for the delivery of financial management consulting services in the eastern region. He also led the firmwide development of the activity-based management practice and was a principal author of *Internal Control—Integrated Framework*. He currently focuses on the consumer products industry and has clients in the public and private sectors. He has held senior management roles in finance and control, distribution, industrial engineering, and division and general management. Prior to his association with Coopers & Lybrand, he was a senior partner and chief financial officer of a major worldwide management consulting firm.

Page xiv, add after entry for Richard S. Wasch:

Serge L. Wind is Assistant Controller for Financial Studies at AT&T, with responsibility for identifying and targeting financial measures, monitoring the capital and investment program, establishing financial targeting via competitor analogs, generating financial models, overseeing transfer pricing, and performing special analytical studies (including analyzing corporate mergers and acquisitions). Mr. Wind holds PhD and BA degrees in statistics and economics, respectively, from Columbia University.

SUPPLEMENT CONTENTS

Note to the Reader: Materials that appear only in the supplement and not in the main volume are indicated by the word (New) after the title.

BUDGETING SHAREHOLDER VALUE (New)

Serge L. Wind

AT&T Company

CONTENTS

11A.1 OVERVIEW OF SHAREHOLDER VALUE. Businesses that want to grow their market shares, or at least to be competitive in their markets, must improve productivity, foster innovation, and strive toward enhanced customer satisfaction. Businesses that want to grow, as manifested by these objectives, must increase investment now for the future.

As the source of much of this required funding, shareholders assess the potential increase in "value" of their investments in a business when deciding to invest or not. This assessment is based on their anticipated return and the risk they associate with it.

It is vital, then, for firms to focus on shareholder satisfaction by understanding what is important to this stakeholder. In this manner, the drivers of intrinsic value (or *shareholder value*) of the firm can be discerned and its value managed.

(a) Purposes.   Shareholder value provides the valuation of a business. The principal purposes of implementing (period) performance measurement of shareholder value are:

- To provide an economic measurement of business performance from the perspective of the shareholder.
- To supplement traditional accounting-based measures of business performance with cash flow valuation.
- To provide proper vehicles for achieving management objectives and decisions—including the planning process, resource utilization, and employee compensation—that drive creation of value.

(b) What Is Shareholder Value?   Return to the share owner is in the form of cash dividends and share price appreciation. Aside from psychic and other nonfinancial attributes of an investment, these are the only returns available to common stockholders.

The value of the shareholder investment emanates from the cash flow generated over the life of the business, assessed with the associated business risk. Thus, shareholder value—the economic measure of the value of a business—is expressed as the sum of future cash flows in today's dollars.

The cash flows are aftertax cash generated each period from the operations of the business, available to all providers of company capital. For a proper analysis of the true worth of cash flows over time, they have to be expressed in terms of today's dollars. (See § 11A.2(b) on the time value of money.)

(c) Why Focus on Cash Flow?   The concept of shareholder value is expressed in terms of cash flows, and is based on current and future cash outflows and inflows from now out to the future. We are adopting an economic perspective, in which cash outlays are delineated as the underlying components of an economic model of valuation. This framework was laid out by Rappaport and others (see Sources and Suggested References).

The emphasis on the discounted cash flow (DCF) approach versus the standard, accounting-based approach also manifests itself in the types of financial measures that are most expressive of economic performance in which investors are interested. Traditional measures, such as earnings per share and returns on equity and operating assets, do not capture all aspects of value creation, including:

- Business risk
- Investor expectations
- Time value of money.

They also often reflect the effects of leverage or the debt ratio, which is the total debt of the firm divided by total capital. Finally, they are single-period, short-term measures. We need to start concentrating on measures, such as the two value-based indicators delineated in the next section, which (unlike accounting earnings) have been found by studies to be highly correlated with stock price, an external indicator of company value.

In their book on valuation, Copeland *et al.* sum it up accurately: "Managers who use the DCF approach to valuation, focusing on long-term cash flow, ultimately will be rewarded by higher share prices. The evidence from the market is conclusive. Naive attention to accounting earnings will lead to value-destroying decisions."[1]

(d) Two Complementary Value-Based Measures.   Two measures of shareholder value will be discussed, because they are related in important ways. Both are value-based measures.

Shareholder value, based on discounted cash flows, measures total long-term value. Long-term valuation is used for:

- Evaluation of investment decisions (both capital projects and acquisitions)
- Assessment of long-term plans and projects
- Economic decision-making.

As we have seen, this measure—the investors' perception of the total worth of a company—is based on all the cash flows to be generated, in order to include all future benefits or returns, as well as costs of all current and future investments and added assets.

For both short-term planning and tracking, *Economic Value Added* or EVA, developed by Stern and Stewart, captures the value created (or depleted) during a period of business activity.[2] (A *period* is a finite time interval, like a year.) Because of its importance to planning and budgeting, EVA is more fully explained in § 11A.3.

Both measures share another key property: they distinguish between operations and financing and measure the effects of only the former in valuation. Inclusion of financing effects (such as interest and number of shares), along with traditional accounting, introduces misleading non-cash-based information in measures like return on equity and EPS.

---

[1]See Tom Copeland, Tim Koller, and Jack Murrin at 94.

[2]Joel Stern and Bennett Stewart defined a form of residual income or Economic Value Added (EVA) in two publications (see Sources and Suggested References).

The critical assertion to be developed for budgeting purposes is that EVA is particularly useful in tracking a plan's contribution to the total shareholder value. The nature of cash flows and their inherent difficulty for budgeting, coupled with the observation that the period cash flow component does not reveal the state of incremental value, combine to favor an added role for EVA. Thus, EVA, apparently relegated to a period measure of value added, takes on an important new role: short-term budget tracker of total value.

11A.2   LONG-TERM VALUATION.   In the last section, we introduced two measures: shareholder value and EVA. Shareholder value is the (long-term) valuation of a company, whereas EVA is a measure of short-term value creation for a period of business activity. Total value, or shareholder value, is always quantified at a point in time (e.g., as of this year), and value is a function of all future time periods.

(a)   Shareholder Value Recapitulation.   Long-term valuation is the best approach to linking shareholder value creation to investment decisions. We have defined *value* as the summation of all projected free cash flows for a business or project, expressed in the equivalent of today's dollars.

Free cash flow represents the aftertax cash generated each period after reinvestment from the operations—not financing—of the business. Reinvestment, from the firm's perspective, consists of net plant adds (or capital expenditures for plant and equipment), changes in operating capital (or changes in receivables and inventory less payables), and investments (or acquisitions, mergers, etc.).

Example of a Statement of Funds Flow		
Operating Income (Before Interest & Taxes)	$895	
+ Other Income (Operating)	112	
- Cash Operating Taxes Paid	(189)	
Income After Cash Taxes (Before Interest)	818	$818
- Additions to Plant Net of Depreciation	(98)	
- Additions to Operating Capital	(34)	
- Additions to Investments	——	
Reinvestment	$(132)	$(132)
Free Cash Flow		$686
= Income After Cash Taxes (before Interest) less Reinvestment		

Exhibit 11A.1.   Definition of free cash flow.

In Exhibit 11A.1, an example is shown of free cash flow, forecasted in terms of future dollars, which must be subsequently "discounted" back to today's dollars.

(b)   Time Value of Money.   The reference to "today's dollars" in § 11A.1(c) is to the economic tenet that "most people prefer to have cash now rather than later," because the cash can now be invested to produce returns unavailable if the cash flow is delayed. The time value of money derives from the cost of foregone opportunities.[3] With the cash flows forecasted in terms of future dollars, the time-value-of-money concept dictates that they must be discounted to equate them to today's dollars, thus providing an estimate of the present value of the business from each period. We will see later that risk as reflected in the cost of capital determines the discount rate.

(c) Cost of Capital.   The rate used to discount future cash flows back to the present for valuation is called the *cost of capital* or *discount rate*. (See Chapter 11 for further discussion on the subject; capital itself is defined in § 11A.3(f).)

The numerical example of discounting assumes negative cash flow of $120 in the first year for an initial project investment, and positive cash flows of $80 in each of the next four years. Although the total of the five years added up to $200 in absolute dollars, that $200 is only equivalent to $110 in today's dollars. The $110 is the *present value.*

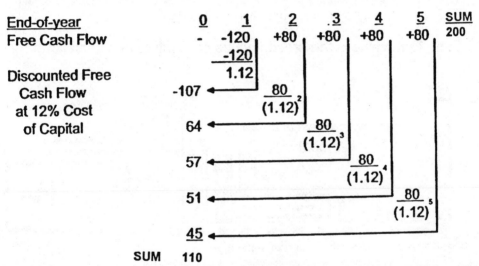

Exhibit 11A.2.   Discounted free cash flow: An example.

The cost of capital is the risk-adjusted opportunity cost for investors, or the minimum required return. The cost of capital represents the average rate of return that investors expect when they decide to invest in a company of a certain risk.

The cost of capital is the weighted average cost of debt capital supplied by bondholders and equity capital supplied by the shareholders. This weighted average cost of capital is often referred to as the *WACC.*

COST OF CAPITAL

Cost of Capital = [After-Tax Cost of Debt x % of Debt in Capital Ratio]

+

[Cost of Equity x % of Equity in Capital Ratio]

---

[3]See Tom Copeland, Tim Koller, and Jack Murrin at 75.

For debt, with interest tax deductible, the aftertax cost of debt is based on the prevailing interest rates (and the effective income tax rate). For equity, the more complicated methods described in Stewart's book[4] are needed to estimate the cost of equity of different companies. Finally, the weights are determined by the corporate objective (or sometimes the actual) debt ratio, usually determined by the treasurer of the company. The cost of equity, in essence, is an estimate of the return required by shareholders for investing in the company's common stock, based on an assessment of the level of risk in the company and other investment alternatives in the marketplace.

(d)   Continuing Value.   As shown in the graphical representations of a long-term value calculation (see exhibit 11A.3), *shareholder value* is the present value of all future free cash flows. For time beyond the explicit planning period (usually 5 or 10 years), a term called *continuing value* captures the remaining future cash flows forecasted into perpetuity. Formulas for continuing value, or residual value, can be found in the valuation book by Copeland, Koller, and Murrin.[5]

• Long-term value is the present value of all future free cash flows

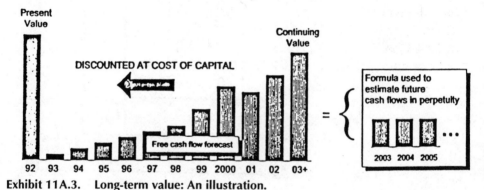

Exhibit 11A.3.   Long-term value: An illustration.

Continuing value, absolutely necessary to compute discounted cash flows, often accounts for more than 70%, and sometime more than 100%, of total value. Moreover, with even near-term forecasts often hard to estimate, the long-term-based continuing value is often difficult to estimate reliably. However, it does represent the premium investors are expecting beyond the explicit planning period.

(e)   Budgeting Implications.   With the most important decisions made by company managers involving value of a pending project or business unit, accountability based on successful implementation is vital. A business plan and budget for the company must reflect the benefits and costs of those projects and business units for which value has been altered.

However, we have seen that valuation is a complex procedure, depending upon multi-years' continuing value, which is determined by imprecise parameters and

---

[4]See Bennett Stewart III, ch. 12, at 431–75 (1990).

[5]See Tom Copeland, Tim Koller, and Jack Murrin at 207–30.

accounts for the majority portion of value, and cash flow projections with start-up problems that reverberate throughout the DCF. Budget practitioners responsible for cash flow items know that actual end-of-year (or start-up) balance sheet items (known only after the budget has been approved) must be taken into account in re-estimating budget-year cash flows (like payables, receivables, additions to plant, and free cash flow).

The complexity and reliability of budgeting and tracking discounted cash flows for even the first few years leaves us amenable to other budgeting notions.

11A.3   ECONOMIC VALUE ADDED (EVA).   We have seen why shareholder value is vital in assessing a company's value over the long term. An ongoing firm needs to be able to check progress as well, and measure increases in value with a short-term measure. EVA, depicted as the most important period measure of value added (or depleted),[6] will also be seen to provide a means for effective budgeting for the DCF measure of shareholder value.

(a)   EVA Overview.   Rather than estimating total value via multi-year cash flows, Economic Value Added measures period value added to or depleted from share-holder value. It relates income statement and balance sheet activity to shareholder expectations, and uses traditional accounting information as a surrogate for cash flows. EVA is more highly correlated with stock price than are traditional measures, according to empirical studies by Stern Stewart.

The EVA formula incorporates earnings, cash income taxes, balance sheet capital, and the cost of capital so that value created is measured (positive value is created when the return on invested capital exceeds the cost of capital). EVA measures oper-ating returns in excess of (or below) the cost of capital. (Financing impacts, such as the tax deductibility of interest expense, are excluded.)

(b)   Example of Value Added Concept.   If you borrow $100 from a bank at a 10% rate for one year, and you earn 12% return on the money through investment or the race track, you have created value for yourself. Your return exceeds the bank's cost to you by two percentage points.

If, however, with the bank cost fixed at 10%, you manage only an 8% return, you have lost money and value by two percentage points.

In an analogous fashion, if the return on invested capital (ROIC) exceeds the cost of capital, value is added. Value is depleted for the period when ROIC is less than the weighted average cost of capital (WACC).

We have already referred to the cost-of-capital component; it is more complex (e.g., two dimensions) than the cost of debt in the example, but plays a role analo-gous to the hurdle rate. (A *hurdle rate* is a threshold value for determining economic acceptance of a project: the return must exceed the hurdle rate.)

We now need to be a bit more precise in defining the return on capital and an explicit EVA equation.

---

[6]See Bennett Stewart III at 3–14 (1986).

(c)   EVA Formula.   Building into the formula the feature that EVA is positive only when the return exceeds the cost of capital, the EVA formula[7] can be written as:

EVA = [Return on Invested Capital - Cost of Capital] x Average Invested Capital

Note that EVA is an actual dollar figure, not a percentage. Its sign indeed depends on the sign of the *spread,* the difference between return and cost of capital (both percentages). Its magnitude or size depends, in large part, on average capital, which is also dollar-denominated. (*Capital* is defined in section 11A.3(f).)

(d)   Implications for Value Creation.   There are three basic means of securing an increase in EVA for the company, as pointed out by Stewart[8]:

An increase in EVA will result:
- If operating efficiency is enhanced
  - Rate of return on existing capital base improves

OR

- If value-added new investments are undertaken
  - Additional capital invested returns more than cost of capital

OR

- If capital is withdrawn from uneconomic activities
  - Capital withdrawn where returns are below cost of capital.

(e)   Components of EVA—Return on Invested Capital.   Return on invested capital (ROIC) in the EVA formula must exceed the cost of capital, the hurdle rate which we have already defined in section 11A.2(c). ROIC, also a percentage, is defined as:

$$\text{ROIC} = \frac{\text{Net operating profit after taxes (NOPAT)}}{\text{Average invested capital}}$$

NOPAT represents posttax earnings before payment of capital costs (i.e., interest and dividends). Essentially, NOPAT includes all revenues and sales net of costs and expenses, plus other operational income, less cash income taxes paid (except for the deductibility of financing-related interest). As such, NOPAT is the right measure to compare pre-capital-cost earnings with investors' costs. Cash taxes are more consistent with cash flow valuation and serve as an appropriate operating driver of EVA, because of comprehensive income taxation employed in accounting.

---

[7]Joel Stern and Bennett Stewart defined *Economic Value Added* and its concept and are responsible for its development into an important model for creating and managing value; the description of EVA in this chapter is based on the value-based framework they generated, as described in two books by Bennett Stewart.

[8]See Bennett Stewart III at 138 (1990).

(f) Components of EVA—Invested Capital. The third component of the EVA formula is average *invested capital*; it also forms the denominator of ROIC. Invested capital represents the cumulative cash invested in the company over time.

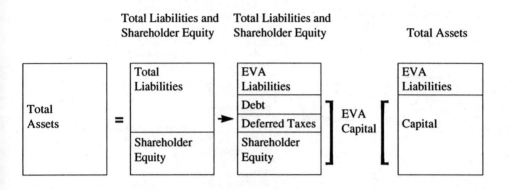

| **Balance Sheet** |

EVA Capital = Total Assets - EVA Liabilities

Exhibit 11A.4.   EVA capital.

EVA capital is defined as the difference between assets and EVA liabilities (excluding debt and deferred taxes), or, equivalently, in terms of the right-hand side of the balance sheet, equity plus equity equivalents (e.g., deferred taxes), plus debt.

In both capital and NOPAT, some corresponding adjustments to each term are required to fit in the EVA formula in § 11A.3(c). Basically, as defined by Stewart,[9] most of these adjustments involve replacing book accounting value with terms that are more cash-flow or economic-based. EVA capital, including the adjustments contained in equity equivalents (e.g., deferred taxes) which convert the standard accounting book value to a form of economic book value, is a truer measure of the cash invested.

(g) Operating Drivers of Value. Key value drivers can be used effectively to include a detailed analysis of the EVA sensitivity to changes in input parameters. Operating drivers include revenue growth, NOPAT margin (i.e., NOPAT divided by revenues), capital turnover (revenues divided by average capital), and some of the other variables from the income statement and balance sheet as depicted in Exhibit 11A.5. For example, inventory turnovers and receivables turnover (or days outstanding) are operating drivers of EVA via capital.

Most of these drivers are related to return on invested capital (ROIC) via duPont decomposition or *ROIC tree*.[10] For example, NOPAT margin, times capital turnover, times the tax factor, equals ROIC.

---

[9]See Bennett Stewart III at 8–13 (1986).

[10]See Tom Copeland, Tim Koller, and Jack Murphy at 125.

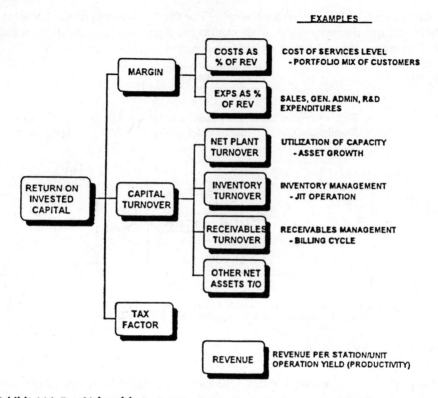

Exhibit 11A.5.   Value drivers.

Financing drivers, distinct from operating drivers, include debt ratio and amounts and costs of capital, but are not controlled by business units or profit centers.

Sensitivity analysis can be applied to valuation and associated decision-making, once the key drivers with the greatest impact on value are identified. For budgeting, the drivers can identify the source of any variance, and can be used for unit trend comparison.

(h)   EVA Attributes.   In describing Economic Value Added, its principal attribute in short-term planning is that it is "the single most important indicator of value creation. . . . EVA measures not only management's ability to manage capital efficiently, but takes into account the magnitude of capital investment as well."[11]

In addition, EVA is an indicator of the company's productivity. We usually think of a firm or industry competing in a market for products and/or services. The conceptual approach of shareholder value suggests that there is another market—the market for investor capital—in which all publicly owned companies must compete simultaneously with its other markets. (We began § 11A.1 with a discussion of the need of companies to be competitive in securing funding.)

As indicated in Exhibit 11A.6 (generated by Deo[12]), the firm strives to attain a sustainable competitive advantage in its markets for its products and services,

---

[11]See Bennett Stewart III at 3–14 (1986).

[12]Adapted from Prakash Deo's unpublished AT&T paper, "Resource Alignment" (1991).

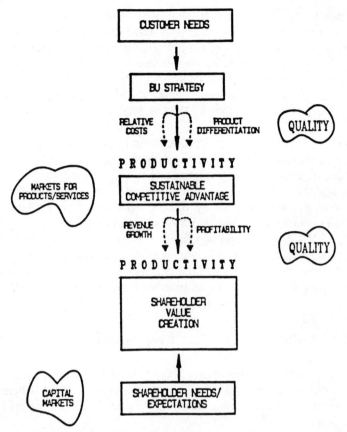

Exhibit 11A.6.   Linking customer and shareholder needs.

through product differentiation, cost minimization, and so forth, to satisfy its customers. Simultaneously, via profitability and revenue growth drivers, the firm satisfies its shareholders' expectations by value creation emanating from its products and services.

Productivity is foremost a measure of ability to create value (or output) in excess of cost (input) of generating it. Two complementary productivity measures are suggested:

1. *Operating margin*—for expense productivity and income statement efficiency
   - Pretax NOPAT divided by total revenues.
2. *Capital turnover*—for capital productivity and balance sheet efficiency
   - Revenue per average capital.

Productivity improvement is year-over-year percentage change in either measure.

Return on invested capital (ROIC) is the joint measure of operating margin and capital productivity; it reveals the company's productivity, as determined by the spread between return on capital and cost of capital, in competition for investor capital.[13]

---

[13]See Bennett Stewart III at 3–14 (1986).

EVA can also be decomposed by disaggregating financial results to delineate the impact of key operating drivers, like revenue growth, pretax profit margin per sales, cash tax rate, net operating capital (NOC) charge and plant, property, and equipment (PPE) charge. These last two drivers, proposed by Stern Stewart, represent the normalized variable (NOC/sales and PPE/sales) times the cost of capital (before taxes), and are derived from viewing EVA as residual income (of earnings in excess of capital charges); that is, EVA = NOPAT - COC x Average Invested Capital.

In the 1992 AT&T Annual Report, CFO Alex Mandl wrote that: "EVA is truly a system of measurement. It supplements traditional accounting measures of performance, giving us additional insight into our business and helping us to identify the factors that affect our performance. We have made it the centerpiece of our 'value-based planning' process. And we are linking a portion of our managers' incentive compensation to performance against EVA targets in 1993."

Moreover, EVA has the important facility of connecting forward-looking valuation to performance evaluation (via actual operating performance) over discrete periods. EVA thereby enables consistent tracking of valuation. However, first, we need to explore in more depth the relationship between the two measures, EVA and shareholder value.

11A.4   COMPLEMENTARY MEASURES OF VALUATION.

(a)   **EVA and Valuation.**   *Shareholder value* was defined in § 11A.2 as the multi-period, long-term valuation of a company (as of a point in time), whereas we have just seen that EVA measures value added to a shareholder's investment for a period (like a year or quarter).

To determine the economic value of an enterprise, operating unit, or project requires a valuation—or all-period analysis—of all future cash flows. Generally, the entity value is the future expected cash flows discounted at a rate (or cost of capital) that reflects the riskiness of the operating cash flow. In particular:

$$\text{VALUE} = \text{PV(FCF)} = \frac{\text{FCF 1}}{1+\text{COC}} + \frac{\text{FCF 2}}{(1+\text{COC})^2} + ...$$

where FCF 1, stands for the free cash flow in period 1 and PV denotes present value or discounted sum.

It is, however, true (only under some conditions) that VALUE also equals the present value of the EVAs plus initial capital CAP:

$$\text{VALUE} = \text{PV(EVA)} + \text{CAP}$$

where

$$\text{PV(EVA)} = \frac{\text{EVA 1}}{1+\text{COC}} + \frac{\text{EVA 2}}{(1+\text{COC})^2} + ...$$

Capital, defined in § 11A.3(f), is not equal to the book value of traditional accounting, but represents economic book value, where adjustments, like the deferred tax reserve, are added to book debt and equity, to allow capital to reflect a more economic and accurate base on which to earn.

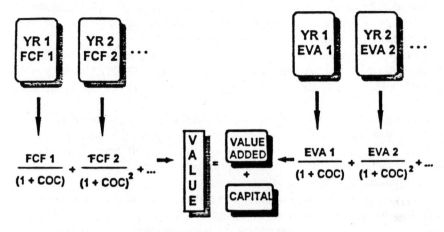

$$PV(FCF) = V = PV(EVA) + CAP$$

Exhibit 11A.7. Valuation.

Although individual-period EVA is usually different from FCF for the same period, under a specific set of assumptions, the two approaches generally yield the same value, i.e.,

$$PV\ (FCF) = PV\ (EVA) + CAP = VALUE,$$

when the amount of initial capital of the firm is added to the discounted EVA (or value added) sum.

This result is important, because it suggests that VALUE may, under certain assumptions, be calculated using EVA components (in place of cash flow) and that the definition of EVA as a period measure of value added yields the same VALUE when a discounted sum of EVA terms is taken. Shareholder value can be expressed in terms of EVA components, too.

For initial implementation, using VALUE (EVA) for valuation is not always recommended, because the set of assumptions for value equality may not be valid in all cases, and FCF-based routines are well established for project valuation in business cases in most firms. The specialized circumstances and assumptions for VALUE equality may not be applicable to the majority of projects and investments of a firm without an adjustment.

Identification and correction of any systematic difference in the VALUE determined by EVA and FCF (usually a function of project timing and start-up assumptions) may be viewed as a transition issue. As implementation takes root, the advantages of consistency—of using EVA as one common measure with a common language and framework, with operating drivers for all planning and budgeting, for both period and total value estimation—may dominate the discomfort of any needed adjustments. In addition, as shown by Worthington,[14] the contribution (as a percent of total value) from EVA continuing value will be less than the percent value attributed to the FCF continuing value; part of this effect is attributable to the role of initial capital in the EVA NPV formulation. Even with reliance on the cash flow approach to calculating value, it would be useful to complement it with the EVA approach to get a different perspective on the components of total value, specifically the value added in the early years and the continuing value.

What is interesting, however, is that the period component of PV (FCF) does not yield any information about value added for the period—but EVA does, by definition. Instead, FCF merely indicates the dependence on parent or external financing.

(b)   Tracking by EVA.   We have already touched upon some difficulties associated with budgeting and tracking valuation by cash flows: the dependence on an intractable continuing value, the impossibility of tracking all years, the shifts in cash flows in the budget year caused by actual prior year-end balance sheet variances, and the lack of information inherent in component cash flows.

A few years of EVA data, on the other hand, indicate how much value has been created by management, and thereby evaluate progress toward shareholder value. When all-period valuation is appropriate, it is recommended that EVA period measures be generated for the first three to five years of analysis, along with the multi-year valuation to supplement the FCF valuation approach and to provide a basis for meaningful budgeting and tracking. As a period performance measure, EVA connects forward-looking valuation to performance evaluation. Because EVA is not a cash flow measure, and because its period interpretation is value-oriented, it greatly facilitates period tracking of value, thereby adding "memory" to the planning process.

(c)   Guide to Appropriate Uses of EVA.   EVA is the best internal, single-period measure of value creation. However, single-period values of EVA are not to be used for critical asset or investment and project evaluation decisions, which are based on long-term value creation potential. Instead, discounted cash flow valuation utilizing net present value (NPV) is mandated for decisions involving multi-period benefits, such as business unit evaluation, lease/buy decisions, mergers and acquisitions, and strategic options assessment. (Subject to the conditions raised in § 11A.4(a), NPV based on EVA could be utilized.)

As discussed in the previous section, EVA, in addition to its primary role, can serve as a complement to discounted cash flow valuation, particularly to gauge the initial impact of the project or investment, and to track.

11A.5   BUDGETING SHAREHOLDER VALUE.   Critical investment decisions, based on long-term valuation, come in several different forms in a typical corporation (as discussed in other chapters of this book). Budgeting of these investments is often spotty, partly because it is difficult to isolate the effects of an investment project embedded in an operating unit's returns.

---

[14]Adapted from Mac Worthington's unpublished AT&T presentation, "Terminal Value Computation in Cash Flow Valuation of Business Opportunities" (1994).

(a) Business Cases.   Business cases are the fundamental support analysis for business decisions involving resource utilization. The business case process, while dealing with periodic projects and investments, must be an integral part of budgeting and planning.

Business cases for R&D and capital (additions to plant, property, and equipment) also serve as the basis for subsequent measurement and tracking actions.

As part of the financial analysis of the project, business case output should exhibit the net present value and other standard measures, as well as the EVA forecasts for the first three to five years. The latter will be compared to actuals to determine if initial additions (or depletions) from value are on schedule. Incremental cash flow effects of investment are represented, along with risks, uncertainty, and alternatives.

Review and approval procedures are usually specified by corporate governance. For example, it is an AT&T corporate requirement that a rigorous business case process drive business investment decisions. Capital investments are further discussed in chapters 19 and 20.

(b) Capital and Investment Programs.   Potential mergers and acquisitions, divestitures, investments, and joint ventures are included in these programs, along with additions to capital (APPE) and additions to finance assets; the latter two categories are included in the program at a more aggregate level.

Consummated ventures should be tracked quarterly, comparing budget and actual values for revenues, EVA, funding, and the like.

Part of the investment analysis is an evaluation of the expected impact on the parent's reported EVA earnings after the acquisition. This assessment is usually more important than the EVA expected from the new entity itself.

Review of major investments will be based on a comparison of original enabling business case expectations with actuals. Again, comparison of the first few years' actuals versus plan EVA values is strongly recommended.

A clear understanding should exist as to the circumstances under which a potential acquisition should be included in the company and entity budgets, rather than merely covered by a separate investment program or business case. Generally, large magnitudes combined with a high degree of uncertainty result in omission of the investment from the budget, or statement of the budget with and without the investment. "Ready for approval" investments are usually reflected in the budget.

(c) Business Plans.   As a part of the annual planning process, each business unit is expected to generate a business plan, consisting in the main of a strategic plan and a financial plan. The first year of the financial plan usually becomes next year's budget. Its monitoring and tracking are discussed in § 11A.5(e).

However, budgeting and tracking should also play a role in subsequent assessments of the business plan. To curtail undue optimism in the late years of the plan (the "hockey stick effect"), financial projections, particularly EVA and revenue, should be monitored and compared to actuals, from the second through tenth years. Such an assessment would conceivably contribute to a greater degree of comfort or discomfort for the attainability of the immediate budget year.

(d)   Resource Allocation.   Based upon resource requirements expressed in the business plans to achieve business strategies and long-term economic profits, senior management makes resource allocation decisions as a step in arriving at a budget for next year and beyond. Strategic considerations are paramount, or at least share equal billing with economic considerations in all resource allocation decisions. A business case analysis of the life-cycle cash flows indicates the economic value of a project.

Economic considerations generally can be assessed by two broad categories: benefit and efficiency measures.[15] Benefit measures reveal the cash benefit from investing in a particular proposal, expressed in dollar terms: measures include shareholder value, net present value (NPV), and discounted cash flows. Efficiency measures, expressed as a percentage, indicate how productive a project is in generating cash, relative to resource costs. A ratio of shareholder value or NPV to the present value of all cash outflows (resource expenditures) is used, as is an internal rate of return. Long-term attractiveness tends to dominate decisions, and capital projects and investments could be ranked by total value (or by value per resource input).

Translation of the consequences of resource allocation must be included in the budget. Economic impact should include impact on EVA and total value. Considerations of cash affordability for the firm must also be evaluated.

(e)   Operating Budget Review.   Once major resource allocation decisions are made, attention falls on the commitment budget. Now period measures, like EVA and FCF, are more important as indicators of value added and current cash flow than total valuation. The year-to-year change in unit EVA is as important a measure as the current level of EVA (and its sign).

The budget should pose a challenge that is achievable. If each operating unit makes its EVA level and that EVA level is viewed as a stepping stone toward maximizing shareholder value over time, the enterprise will be successful.

A budget (by year, quarter, and, usually, month) consists of parts or all of an income statement, balance sheet, funds flow, and measures (particularly, the explicit commitment measures to which compensation is tied). In this budgeting mode, EVA is the best measure.

(f)   Monthly Actuals Reporting.   Key measures compared by unit and month for budget versus actual and budget versus last year's period should include EVA, FCF, and revenue. EVA can be decomposed into its operating drivers—revenue growth, NOPAT margin, and capital turnover—and the respective variances compared to better understand shortfalls. As EVA is implemented in the company, additional critical information can be shown, such as variance in the EVA operating drivers, discussed in section 11A.3(g).

Exhibit 11A.8 displays useful information for management of budget/actual differences in EVA, underlying data, and drivers. Consolidated EVA is also shown in internal company reports as a sum of entity EVAs for actual and budget, enabling identification of entity shortfalls. A modified tree diagram, like Exhibit 11A.5, displays more value drivers, to assess the principal source of actual/budget variance.

---

[15]Adapted from Harish Chandra's unpublished AT&T memo, "Resource Allocation" (1993).

($)	Actual	Budget	Difference
Operating Income	133	139	(6)
EVA Adjustments	(11)	(9)	(2)
Adjusted Operating Income	122	130	(8)
Cash Taxes Paid	(35)	(37)	2
	----	----	----
NOPAT	87	93	(6)
Avg. Invested Capital	579	599	(20)
EVA	20	24	(4)

EVA Drivers Impact		
Change in NOPAT		(6)
Change in Adj. Operating Income	(8)	
Change in Cash Taxes Paid	2	
Change in Avg. Capital @ 11.5% Cost of Capital		2
Change in EVA		(4)

Exhibit 11A.8.   EVA year-to-date results.

11A.6   SUMMARY OF BUDGET VALUATION TECHNIQUES.   Effectively managing and measuring value calls for different, although complementary, techniques depending upon the intended use and the associated time period required. For decisions involving long-term value creation potential, the all-period FCF valuation should be utilized to estimate shareholder value. However, for budgeting purposes, the EVA annual component is particularly valuable in budgeting as a measure of value created in a period. It indicates how much value is to be created from capital by management, and thereby evaluates progress toward the all-period shareholder value.

For a single period, EVA is the best measure of value creation, and EVA should be monitored and tracked for budgeting.

Valuation must be closely linked to single-period measures of value created. When all-period valuation is required (e.g., business cases), it is recommended that EVA period measures be generated for the first three to five years of analysis to provide a basis for meaningful budgeting and tracking.

We have seen that EVA is particularly well suited to discern the drivers of EVA budget variances, especially to determine whether the income statement or balance sheet is variance-causative.

Adding measures like EVA to budget and planning processes has some practical consequences, which have been very positive. In particular, attention must be paid to balance sheets, as well as just income statements.

The use of EVA has also aided the establishment of market-facing business units and strategic business units by prescribing a meaningful sufficient set of financials and an associated measure of value-added that enables close scrutiny of the true financial performance of these discrete entities. Thus, adoption of EVA is seen as a boon to driving financials to the smallest revenue-generating units, because cash taxes and capital on the balance sheet, in addition to standard profitability, are required components at a business unit or strategic business unit level (usually characterized by separate markets, customers, products/services, competitors, and so on).

SOURCES AND SUGGESTED REFERENCES

Copeland, Tom, Koller, Tim, and Murrin, Jack, *Valuation—Measuring and Managing the Value of Companies,* John Wiley & Sons, New York, 1990.

Rappaport, Alfred, *Creating Shareholder Value,* The Free Press, New York, 1986.

Stewart, G Bennett III, *The Quest for Value,* HarperCollins, New York, 1990.

Stewart, G. Bennett III, *Stern Stewart Corporate Finance Handbook,* Stern Stewart Management Services, New York, 1986.

CHAPTER 15

SALES AND MARKETING BUDGET (Revised)

R. Malcolm Schwartz

CONTENTS

Pages 15 • 1 to 15 • 16, delete entire chapter and replace with:

15.1 INTRODUCTION. The sales and marketing budget is an important link with all other budgets. To make this link effective, the budget system should be based on a sound understanding of the vision, culture, and objectives of the organization; on an awareness of the relationships among business processes and with other business functions; on the ability to use external information about competitors, customers, suppliers, and public policy; and on good judgment.

The importance of these factors suggests that the sales and marketing budget process should be discussed broadly and not merely in terms of how related data should be entered, stored, and printed from a computer system. Therefore, this chapter concentrates on the following subjects:

- An overview of the budget process
- Special budgeting problems
- Pertinent tools
- Unique aspects of some industries

15.2 OVERVIEW OF THE BUDGET PROCESS. The sales and marketing budget process links to product, channels of distribution, and profit a group of largely discretionary expenses that focus on customers' acceptance—on the downstream components of the value chain. Most firms try to sell profitably what customers want, that is, what the market will bear. As a result, the sales and marketing budget is a means of integrating the functional plans as well as the process capabilities of an organization. It is important that the budget be controlled because marketing expenses, which are not only largely discretionary but also can be changed dramatically as to priorities and mix, can be misdirected quite easily.

As a result, a budget process should be in place that can be integrated with other plans and that can provide useful analyses to support the judgments of marketing planners.

(a) A Link Between Strategic and Other Functional Plans. The sales and marketing budget provides a link between the business strategy and other functional plans. The sales budget defines the level and mix of projected product and services offerings, as well as such support costs as sales organization expense and trade promotion and education programs. This information generally is developed to be consistent with the organization's overall strategic plan and to provide more detailed information for the planning period covered by the overall budget.

Much sales information traditionally is "top line" (that is, it is presented at the top of a profit and loss statement): the identification of short-term activity that it provides links the strategic plan to the budgets of other functions that support achieving the intended operating level. These other budgets include:

- **Operations (sourcing, conversion, and physical distribution).** Factors that are affected include inventory and service levels, replenishment techniques, production mix, and lengths of production runs.
- **Research and Development.** Replacing products over their life cycles, anticipating customers' wants and needs and competitors' actions, and taking advantage of technological developments should help to identify priorities for development projects as well as the funding levels.
- **Administration.** A number of these support functions—ranging from clerical activities, such as order entry and customer service, to legal specialists—can be influenced by the sales budget.
- **Capital Investment.** The needs for facilities, tooling, and equipment should be coordinated with sales activity.

- **Cash.** Inventory, accounts receivable, and accounts payable all can be affected by the sales budget.

The marketing budget in turn relates in two ways to sales plans. First, it can be driven by sales plans, as when higher volumes can cause greater expenditures for cooperative advertising. Second, it can be used to drive sales plans, as when promotional activities are planned to support sales growth or mix. The overall sales and marketing budget is therefore a means of integrating a number of plans to the strategy of the organization.

Today, many organizations think of this integration in process rather than functional terms. In such cases, plans and budgets may be process-focused rather than function-focused. A typical framework of processes and the business cycles they encompass might include:

- **Customer Management**—from offering to selling products and services
- **Product Management**—from planning through discontinuing product offerings
- **Supply Chain**—from receiving demand signals through delivering products and services, including sourcing and conversion activities
- **Development**—from considering innovations through applying them
- **Support**—all infrastructure activities.

Whether a company takes a functional or a process view, the sales and marketing—or customer and product—planning is an important link between strategy and business activities.

(b)   Discretionary Expenses.   In addition to consideration of product, price, promotion, and volume, the sales and marketing budget deals with a number of expenses that are largely discretionary. Sales budgeting deals with issues such as what products are to be sold, what prices are to be charged, how customer loyalty can be encouraged, and how much volume should result.

The marketing portion of the budget considers what resources are to be used—and in what mix—to move products from the firm to its customers. Major elements of the marketing budget include:

- **Selling**—which may involve direct selling through various media, an employed sales force, sales representatives, or some combination.
- **Sales Promotion**—which often includes a combination of price and premium programs, trade shows, store fixtures, coupons, sponsorship, and the like.
- **Advertising**—which may concentrate on the image of the firm, a product line, or a brand; which may be national, regional, local, or customer-specific; and which can use various media.
- **Product Development**—which some firms consider a marketing expense, particularly for short-term efforts; and which can include new features, packaging changes, new products, and the like.
- **Customer Service**—which includes both warranty and out-of-warranty support, education, training, complaint handling, and a variety of other services.

- **Physical Distribution**—which some organizations treat as a marketing expense; and which may be handled centrally or may be spread through the regions served; other discretionary factors include how goods are shipped and whether the firm elects to use its own resources, distributors, or public warehouses.

The marketing budget considers what mix and levels of these elements will be used. Therefore the budget process should enable analyses that consider trade-offs, priorities, and contingent actions in support of the eventual agreed plan.

(c) Operating Factors. The budgeting process should consider a number of operating factors that shape the expenses planned for sales and marketing.

There are several different ways in which the levels of the various elements of marketing expense can be analyzed and targeted; these include historical trends, standards or benchmarks, and operating factors.

Historical trends can be applied rather simply; for example, if sales are planned to increase by 10%, then advertising can be increased by the same percentage. This approach takes little effort, but it assumes that prior levels of expenses were effective, that there are no benefits from growth, and that similar levels of expense will be needed in the future.

Standards—usually in the form of typical levels of expenses for certain industries—may be available, but because most firms have different objectives and operations they can be hard to apply. Furthermore, an industry-wide benchmark can be too broad to have useful application. At the least, if benchmarks are used, the underlying practices should be understood and applicable. Standards for marketing expenses are usually more effective for checking if the plan varies from industry practice—and for being able to understand why and the associated risks—than as a means of developing the budget.

When developing the marketing budget, it is probably more useful to analyze the underlying operating factors that drive market performance than to rely on history or on benchmarks. Examples of such drivers include:

- Market share
- New account and customer retention rates
- Customer ordering patterns (size, frequency, and mix)
- Value of the customer and value to the customer
- Competitive position
- Impact of past promotions
- Costs to acquire an account
- Sales call patterns

Exhibit 15.1 shows the impact of these and other factors on sales and marketing costs. By reviewing the factors that are important to the firm and how they relate to performance, the marketing planner likely will be able to make better recommendations regarding the amount and mix of marketing expense elements.

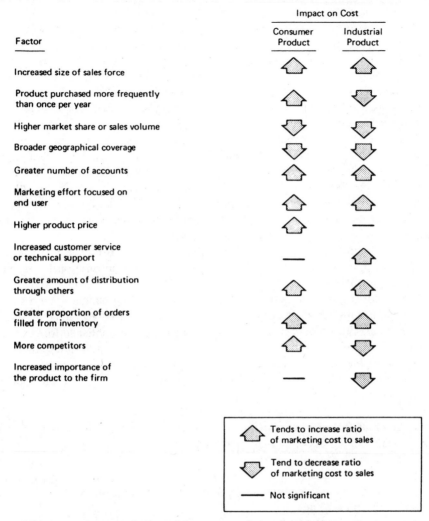

Factor	Impact on Cost	
	Consumer Product	Industrial Product
Increased size of sales force	⬆	⬆
Product purchased more frequently than once per year	⬆	⬇
Higher market share or sales volume	⬇	⬇
Broader geographical coverage	⬇	⬇
Greater number of accounts	⬆	⬆
Marketing effort focused on end user	⬆	⬆
Higher product price	⬆	—
Increased customer service or technical support	—	⬆
Greater amount of distribution through others	⬆	⬆
Greater proportion of orders filled from inventory	⬆	⬆
More competitors	⬆	⬇
Increased importance of the product to the firm	—	⬇

⬆ Tends to increase ratio of marketing cost to sales

⬇ Tend to decrease ratio of marketing cost to sales

— Not significant

Exhibit 15.1. Impact of selected factors on sales and marketing cost.

Therefore, the budgeting system should include operating information as well as cost information.

(d) Culture and Management Style. The organizational architecture and the priorities that underlie the sales and marketing budget should fit with management style as well as with other processes. Because it is a means of integrating plans throughout the organization and the actions that result, it is important to consider issues of culture and management style when constructing the sales and marketing budget. These issues deal with responsibility, authority, accountability, and empowerment; the importance of sole contributors or teams; how decisions get made; and the like. Culture issues also must consider information management—efficiency, cost, integrity, and the like—so that actions can focus on what should be done and not on whose information is correct.

An important culture issue is goal-setting: some executives prefer to hold managers responsible for the actions that they directly control, whereas others want managers to be aware also of the indirect consequences. For example, promotional activity directly affects prices and volumes and may indirectly affect the costs of order entry, credit, and accounts receivable, among other activities. In dealing with these different styles of relating responsibility to the budget structure, two approaches are used, the direct and the full cost methods, the concepts of which have been discussed in earlier chapters.

The direct cost method relates to products only those costs that are expressly associated with them; in addition to product costs, these may include elements of the sales and marketing budget, such as promotional expense, cooperative advertising programs, and the like. The full cost method relates all costs to products by allocating indirect cost elements; as a result, product profitability can be measured in the same way that business profitability is measured. The direct cost method is often supported today by activity-based costing principles.

In the direct cost method, which is simpler from a performance management viewpoint, product performance is measured in terms of contribution to business overhead and profit.

Whatever costing method is used, the sales and marketing budget system should be coordinated with other systems. For example, the chart of accounts should be used effectively. With proper planning, subaccounts can be established for products, salespersons, customer classifications, promotional programs, and other categories that are useful for planning and control. Just as expenses can be related to the accounting system, operating factors can be related to other parts of the management information system.

(e) Incremental Planning and Analysis.   Assuming that the sales and marketing budget is used to integrate other plans and budgets, and that the revenue and expense information is built up from operating factors, another major system feature is to allow for incremental planning. Depending on the business and industry, planning increments might include geographic regions, channels of distribution, classes of customers, and product lines.

When plans are developed incrementally, adjustments can be more focused during the review process. Key steps in budgeting incrementally include the following:

- Identify the increments
- Analyze the related operating factors
- Develop the sales and marketing plan for each increment
- Extend each increment to revenues and expense
- Sum the increments to form a base budget
- Review the base budget for consistency with the firm's strategy, for profit, for an assessment of competitive actions, and for overall affordability
- Adjust the base budget as needed and at the level of the individual increments
- Test the adjusted base budget for profit sensitivity to different levels of expense.

Finally, when the optimal incremental programs have been budgeted, and at levels that should generate desired profits, the budget can be approved and a road map will have been provided for sales and marketing efforts. This approach enables the linking of "top-down" and "bottom-up" budgeting, focused at the sales and marketing decisions. Exhibit 15.2 provides an overview of this process.

15.3   SPECIAL BUDGETING PROBLEMS.   Because marketing expenditures are so discretionary and can be combined in so many different ways, it can be difficult to develop meaningful levels of expense for each element of cost. During the budgeted period, it can also be difficult to control expense levels and to adapt them to changing circumstances. This section reviews some of the more general aspects of these problems as they relate to the major cost elements.

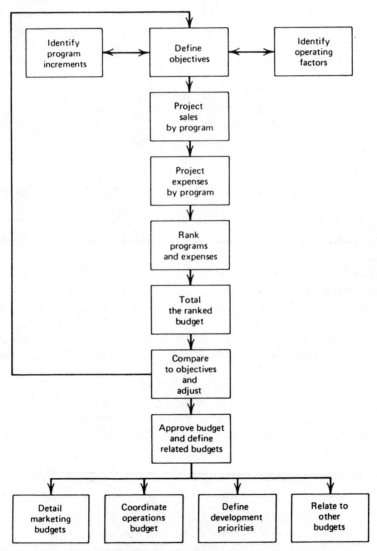

Exhibit 15.2.   Approach to incremental budgeting.

(a) Pricing Adjustments.   Planned pricing and any adjustments need to be budgeted if future revenues are to be attained and controlled.

Prices are usually developed both in relationship to costs and in response to competition. For products that have leading positions in the market, prices may be based on value to the customer.

New products can be difficult to price. At the time of initial market entry, prices are sometimes set close to cost to achieve desired volume and market share. After these goals are attained, prices might be adjusted. During the same period—as volume is growing—product costs could be declining; as a result, prices could be kept stable and profits would increase.

When prices are declining, it may be necessary to plan additional discounts. These usually can be better controlled in many companies' systems than outright price reductions because they can be recorded and tracked as expenses. Some companies overcome this limitation by tracking both standard and realized prices.

For any product for which a price change is planned, it is useful to control this by budgeting at the base price and then showing for each period in the budget the pricing adjustments that are to be made.

(b) Selling Expense.   Selling expense includes a number of cost elements, such as salary, commissions, training, and salespersons' expenses. These costs often are associated with different sales forces for regions, classes of customers, or groups of products. Selling expense should be budgeted incrementally in ways that enable future analyses; as examples:

- Firms with large in-store sales forces may want to budget and report selling expense by department, by transaction, by day, and by time of day; data such as these enable correlating store staffing with service levels.
- Firms whose sales forces cover wide geographical areas may want to compare the times to call on customers in urban and rural areas.
- Mail order firms usually want to evaluate selling expense geographically (zip codes are often used) and by the source of the sale (which could be from a specific list of names, from particular advertising copy, or from a media placement).

The kinds of monitoring analyses that will be needed should be identified as the budget is being assembled so that techniques for reporting and control can be established.

(c) Sales Promotion Expense.   Too often, sales promotions are undertaken to increase sales without sufficient attention to planning and controls. Lack of control can be found with sales personnel as well as with customers, as seen in the following examples:

- The internal auditor for a household products firm found that some promotional fixtures never had been placed in stores, and yet sales representatives were receiving commissions approved by the sales manager.
- When a mail order firm revised its customer list programs, it found that one customer had made a number of minor changes in his name and address to obtain more than $10,000 worth of free promotional merchandise.

Because there are few industry standards for sales promotion expense, each firm needs to use its own track record to determine what is effective. Records should be kept—and incorporated into budgets and controls—for the relationships among volume, product, media, and promotional devices. Later promotions can be correlated to benchmarks that are developed, and variances can be analyzed, as misredemption or promotional losses, as examples.

In addition to incremental planning and control of merchandise, the expenses for premiums and coupons and other elements of sales promotion also should be planned and controlled incrementally. As examples:

- Trade shows and exhibits often are planned and controlled for each instance, and analyzed in relationship to sales activity generated.
- Samples and giveaways are usually controlled by salespersons, to evaluate any unusual rates of usage.
- Fixtures often are controlled as if they were inventory, and may need accountability by both salesperson and customer.

(d) Advertising Budget.   Advertising often appears to be discretionary to management and can become one of the first elements of expense to be reduced in bad times. It therefore is important to be able to assess the effectiveness of advertising. Copy, timing, media, and placement can be important factors. The budget should be assembled so that advertising expense and sales activity can be correlated. Similarly, tests of geographical coverage, copy, and the like need to be controlled.

Control can be exercised by having the advertising organization develop standards (examples can include recall, impact, or sales percentages) for effectiveness, and then conduct tests regularly to measure that impact. Advertising expenditures by product are often published (for example, in *Advertising Age*), so that a firm's expenditures can also be compared to these external benchmarks.

Dealer cooperative advertising presents another problem in planning and control that can influence both the design of a budget system and the process of budgeting. Cooperative claims should be verified by tearsheets for print advertising and by invoices for television and radio. As a consequence, a subsystem is needed, by dealer, in regard to claimable amounts, claims pending, and claims approved and paid. The claimable amounts, which are usually based on purchases of a given product or products for a specified period, should be tracked to establish the potential expense, although actual claims paid are often much less.

Even with the use of benchmarks and analyses to explain what advertising is important and why, it still remains a discretionary expense. Occasionally, when management attempts to reduce advertising expense, it finds that commitments already have been made for future expenditures. Therefore the budget system—and the resulting controls—should incorporate plans for the timing and amount of commitments as well as expenditures.

(e) Product Development Costs.   Marketing management uses product development to procure new styles of packaging, new features, and the like. Such procurements can be internal, or items may be purchased from suppliers. In any case, development efforts and their associated costs are best controlled by project. A product development project subsystem can be used to link the research and development budget with the marketing expense budget.

(f) Customer Service Expenses.   The influence of consumer price and value sensitivities, and the needs for differentiation in the marketplace, have caused warranty and other service programs to be expanded. Recalls and replacements have become more common. More staff is being used to answer consumers' questions, and more information is available, in return, to shape product and marketing plans.

As a result, new methods are being used to plan and control customer service expenses. Warranty expenses have usually been planned as a percentage of sales, but today more attention is being given to relating warranty expense to particular products and their sources. Recall expenses can be projected from Total Quality Management programs, and from the statistical process control activities that tend to follow. Replacement expenses can be estimated from failure rate percentages related to the product and developed in the quality control laboratory.

Comparative trends of expenses on these elements of cost should be monitored, and should be used to:

- Adjust the budget
- Provide reserves on actual performance
- Focus development activities
- Direct quality assurance actions.

(g) Physical Distribution.   Physical distribution involves market-responsive trade-offs between service and cost. Service levels should be planned and performance monitored. Often, service can provide an important competitive advantage when price, product features, and the like are not highly differentiable among competitors.

Higher levels of inventory usually accompany better service, and with the annual costs to carry inventory often approaching 25% of inventory value, it is important to ensure that service is worth the cost. In many cases, service can be improved with the same or a reduced inventory level by planning and controlling where the inventory is located across the overall supply chain and for what product, by improving demand communications (using point-of-sale, or POS, information, for example), and by synchronizing the sourcing, conversion, and delivery activities.

As a consequence, the sales and marketing system should be linked to the inventory control system, and through it, to manufacturing and purchasing. Marketing information is needed by product and location; service as well as cost data should be planned, reported, and analyzed. A system of this sort provides the performance benchmarks related to objectives that can help to resolve the usual conflicts about inventory among marketing, finance, and operating managers.

15.4   PERTINENT TOOLS.   There are a number of techniques that are helpful in budgeting and controlling sales and marketing expense. These include:

- Product life-cycle analyses
- Marginal analysis
- Breakeven analysis

- Forecasting
- Sensitivity techniques
- Bracket budgeting
- Pricing techniques
- Performance tests.

This section discusses some of the key features of these techniques.

(a) Analysis of Product Life Cycles. Each phase of a product's life cycle presents different budgeting concerns, ranging from early investment requirements and inventory to "fill the pipeline" to later issues of price and of product discontinuance. Methods need to be established in advance to determine when a product is moving from one phase to another so that:

- Strategies and budgets can be adjusted.
- Agreement can be reached on whether to extend the product's life.
- Planning guidelines can be set on removing the product from the market.

A product life cycle is usually longer than the budget period, so a product plan should be developed that relates to a series of budgets. The product plan should include information on the competitive environment because:

- Little competition may relate to the introductory phase.
- New competitors may indicate the beginning of the growth phase.
- A variety of differentiated products often shows the maturity phase.
- Identical competitive products may point to the decline phase.

The technique of monitoring products' life cycles can help to direct development efforts for differentiating and improving products and thus for extending their lives.

(b) Marginal Analysis. Marginal analysis, which has been discussed previously, can be helpful for cost allocation. Different geographical or sales categories can be tested so that incremental revenue less incremental cost derived from the last unit sold in each area is equal. To illustrate marginal analysis, an advertising budget can be assigned to two categories, and then $1.00 can be transferred from the first to the second; if profit increases, then the transfer is worthwhile and should be continued until no change in profit occurs.

(c) Breakeven Analyses. Breakeven analysis, which was discussed in chapter 8 and chapter 10, requires knowledge of fixed and variable costs and of contributions for individual products. With these data, the breakeven point can be calculated. The result of such an analysis may indicate that increasing the sales of selected products will help to cover fixed costs; if so, the sales and marketing budget should focus on efforts to support that objective.

(d)   Forecasting Techniques.   Most firms forecast by extending historical data for themselves, for competitors, and/or for the overall industry. Some companies incorporate economic data, or have determined that there are leading indicators that help in forecasting sales, such as new home starts for heavy appliances or marriage rates for tableware. Economic data can be obtained from government publications, trade journals, industry associations, consulting firms, and banks; computer programs can be used to test historical correlations.

Many firms rely heavily on internal data for forecasting sales. Using regression analysis or other statistical techniques, a series of internal and external factors can be selected and tested to determine if they help to predict sales. Often, firms rely on simpler statistical techniques, such as moving averages.

Of course, because forecasts are never precise, it is best to rely on actual demand signals for operational and tactical actions. For planning, however, some form of forecasting usually will be needed. To deal with the uncertainty of forecasts, it is useful to consider a range of possible outcomes, with related assumptions, impacts, and probabilities of occurrence.

(e)   Sensitivity Analysis.   Sensitivity analysis can be used, for example, to simulate best, likely, and worst cases before they occur. Relationships must first be understood between the conditions that are to be tested and their effects on sales, costs, and profits; these conditions could include changes in:

- The market, such as overall demand or competitive share
- The economy, such as monetary or fiscal policies or local business conditions
- The environment, including changes in life style or demographic shifts.

Sensitivity analysis is often coupled with probability techniques to answer "what if" questions. For example, a firm might want to know the impact of interest rates on cash flow—for example, at 5% interest a particular project is profitable, but at 12% interest it is not. The project can be analyzed for a series of interest rates, and a probability can be assigned to each one. An overall expected benefit thus can be determined, as illustrated in exhibit 15.3.

(f)   Bracket Budgeting.   Bracket budgeting is a form of built-in contingency planning. Expenses are developed at higher and lower levels (plus or minus 10%, for example) than the base budget, and sales that are likely to result are then forecast. At a later date, if sales were to rise and management should act to maintain the higher level, the likely impact on expenses would already be understood.

If the sales budget were not achieved, the bracket budget gives management a sense of the profit impact, and a contingency plan can be installed quickly. A detailed discussion of this subject is found in chapter 26.

(g)   Tactical and Strategic Pricing Techniques.   Various techniques are used for tactical pricing, which is usually practiced in times of static market conditions and growing demand. These include cost-based pricing, reaction to competitors, and penetration pricing.

Cost-based pricing rests on sound knowledge of all costs as well as effective management of costs that are allocated among products. Reaction to competitive moves has been used by smaller firms who must respond—often by charging less—to industry leaders. Penetration pricing occurs when a firm consciously reduces its usual profit objective to increase market share or to emphasize profitable aftermarket sales (selling razors to sell blades, as an example).

Strategic pricing is appropriate with slow-growing economies, changing demand levels, and stiff competition. This techniques often relates to value as perceived by the customer. For example, reformulating a product by removing an additive that did not have broad appeal could enable a price reduction with a concomitant sales gain. Strategic pricing can also relate to the pace of technological change or to the uniqueness of the product.

The Problem

Invest $33,000.

Positive cash flow is projected by year at $10,000, $10,000, $8,000, $7,000, and $5,000.

Current interest rate is 5%.

Will the investment be worthwhile if interest rates go higher?

The Sensitivity Analysis[a]

Year	Cash Flow	5%	6%	8%	10%
1	$10,000	$9,524	$9,434	$9,259	$9,091
2	10,000	9,070	8,900	8,573	8,264
3	8,000	6,910	6,717	6,350	6,010
4	7,000	5,759	5,545	5,145	4,781
5	5,000	3,918	3,737	3,403	3,105
Total cash in		$35,181	$34,333	$32,730	$31,251
Cash out		(33,000)	(33,000)	(33,000)	(33,000)
Net present value		$2,181	$1,333	$ (270)	$(1,749)

Conclusion: If interest rates approach 8%, do not do the project.

What is management's judgment on the likelihood?

The Expected Benefit Analysis

Year	Probability by Interest Rate				Adjusted Net Present Value
	5%	6%	8%	10%	
1	80%	20%	—	—	$9,506
2	80%	20%	—	—	9,036
3	—	50%	30%	20%	6,466
4	—	50%	30%	20%	5,272
5	—	50%	30%	20%	3,511
Estimated cash in					$33,791
Cash out					(33,000)
Net present value					$ 791

Conclusion: If management's judgment about interest rates is correct, do the project.

[a]Using present value technique.

Exhibit 15.3.   Example of sensitivity analysis.

- For a market in which technology is expected to change in five years, product durability could be designed to that period, and price reduced accordingly.
- Unique product or service features—or the level of technical support—may enable product differentiation and value-added pricing; alternatively, store-branded products can be priced lower because they use available capacity and require less marketing expense.

In any regard, the pricing techniques that are used can influence the structure of the sales and marketing budget as well as the related systems and reports. Emphasis on cost-based pricing, for example, requires more complete cost portrayals, more emphasis of cost differentiation by product, and sensible rules for allocating fixed costs; activity-based costing is a useful supportive approach.

(h)   Testing Actual Performance.   Whatever specialized techniques are used for planning and evaluation, the system should have the ability to provide feedback. Plans to increase or decrease expense should be tested in controlled situations to measure the impact on sales.

For example, results of a market test should be compared to plan, and the budget system should be adapted accordingly. The capability of analyzing controlled changes will enable the extrapolating of results to later budget periods.

15.5   UNIQUE ASPECTS OF SOME INDUSTRIES.   Just as each firm is distinctive, so many industries have different characteristics that cause different approaches to sales and marketing budgeting. This section identifies some features of selected industries—namely, consumer packaged goods, industrial products, retailing, and banking—to illustrate some of the differences. These four industries were selected to illustrate differences resulting from products or services, from customers, and from method of distribution.

(a)   Consumer Packaged Goods Firms.   Budgets for this type of firm often begin with stated goals for market share. Strategies for product, distribution, price, copy, media, promotion, special programs, and volume are formed to reach these goals. Costs are assigned to each strategy and, along with expected volume, are compared to profit objectives. Expense levels are generally determined by a combination of experience and test marketing; external standards are rarely used to determine expense levels, but benchmarks are often used to test the reality and risk in the plan.

The budget usually links other functional plans. Marketing efforts are geared to the profit objective. The manufacturing plan provides cost information that must be assumed by marketing management. The product manager (in the marketing organization) often controls the research and development budget. Because plans are linked and the overall effort is market-driven, the marketing plan often includes a section that identifies where and how the budget should be changed if conditions warrant.

Selling efforts are often important and the sales force can be large. Pressure therefore can be created to price low, to provide substantial promotional activity, and to structure large incentive compensation programs. The trade (the direct customer) also can come to expect continuing promotions, cooperative allowances, and the like. The budget system enables management to plan and evaluate these activities and to make sure that they really are productive.

(b)   Industrial Products Firms.   The sales force is the key element in the selling of industrial products; hence the budget should be geared to provide the mix of expenses that will best support that selling effort. Underlying policies are important, such as warranty, prepaid freight, and trade-in allowance. These are often developed more to fit the company objectives than to imitate competitors' policies. Costs generally are influenced by the policies that are set. This individualized approach precludes the use of external standards to set expense levels, so an internal data base is important. Again, benchmarking and analyzing best practices are increasing in use.

Sales forecasts also are usually based on internal data. Firms with long order lead-in times can analyze their backlogs or, in some cases, the progress against completion of large jobs. Share of market information is seldom used because share tends to remain stable or is less meaningful. Most sales projections involve collecting and interpreting historical and competitive data.

The budget is usually linked with the purchasing and manufacturing plans. Occasionally, too little attention is given to linkages with service and applications engineering budgets. Sales personnel can overpromise service or product adaptability, and the support functions have difficulty in delivering what was promised; effective planning and control, coupled with procedural guidelines, can prevent problems of this sort.

(c)   Retailing.   Whereas the focus for consumer packaged goods is on the market and for industrial products is on the selling effort, for retail the budgeting focuses on the merchandise—what to sell and how it is to be sold. Key factors include fashion trends, the cycle of selling seasons, and the pressure to move inventory.

Forecasts are often quite detailed, in some cases down to item by store. Forecasts are coordinated between buyers of merchandise and store managers—the first reflects fashion trends and the second relates the merchandise to local conditions. Expenses are usually projected by store and sometimes by department. Various trade associations publish extensive data on expenses by merchandise category, by store size, and by volume. Pricing involves target and historic markups by product line, adjusted for inventory movement and promotional activity.

The budget is closely linked to buying activities. Usually, a buyer can commit only up to an inventory limit (called an "open to buy"), so merchandise must be sold to enable future merchandise to be bought. Open to buy is carefully planned and monitored. The expense budget is controlled by store management; if sales are low, steps usually are taken to reduce advertising expense or the sales force.

(d)   Banking.   Bank budgeting focuses on budgeting the differential between the costs to obtain and the costs to lend funds. Key elements of the budget include projecting availability of funds, interest rates, loan demand, deposit demand, and operating expenses.

Economics information and knowledge of the business environment are important factors in budgeting. In banking, sales information is in terms of the amount and types of loans, the interest rates that pertain, the timing of repayment, and likely loan losses.

Sophisticated forecasting and control techniques are used in regard to economic conditions, interest rates, loan demand, and consumer needs. Banks' marketing departments use research techniques (those that are traditionally used by consumer products firms) to evaluate new financial services products.

15.6 SUMMARY. The sales and marketing budget is a key integrative device in many industries. It relates the firm's strategy to operating plans for various functions. It is a means with which to deal with a mass of external and internal data. It should link a number of subsystems for controlling elements of marketing expense and for evaluating the strategy for a product over its life cycle. Therefore, developing and maintaining a sales and marketing budget system requires a broad understanding of the overall business and its strategy and needs.

SOURCES AND SUGGESTED REFERENCES

Ahadiat, Nasrollah, "Sales Forecasting and Cash Budgeting for Automotive Dealerships," *Journal of Busines Forecasting,* Vol. 11, Issue 11, Fall 1992.

Andris, A., Mantrala, Murali, K., Prabhakant, Sinha, and Zoltners, "Impact of Resource Allocation Rules on Marketing Investment-Level Decisions and Profitability," *Journal of Marketing Research,* Vol. 29, Issue 2, May 1992.

Anonymous, "Budgeting for the Agency Sales Force," *Agency Sales Magazine,* Vol. 20, Issue 5, May 1990.

Anonymous, "The Road to Upfront: Beverages," *Mediaweek,* Vol. 3, Issue 20, May 17, 1993.

Anonymous, "Sound Budgeting Can Help Control Costs and Increase Profits; Five Basic Ways to Budget for Your Advertising Needs," *Profit-Building Strategies for Business Owners,* Vol. 22, Issue 4, April 1992.

Anonymous, "You Said It: How Do You Balance Your Sales Budget?" *Sales & Marketing Management,* Vol. 144, Issue 11, September 1992.

Anonymous, "1991 Sales Manager's Budget Planner," *Sales & Marketing Management,* Vol. 143, Issue 7, June 17, 1991.

Anonymous, "1993 Sales Manager's Budget Planner," *Sales & Marketing Management,* Vol. 145, Issue 7, June 28, 1993.

Book, Joel, "Building a Marketing Info System," *Agri Marketing,* Vol. 29, Issue 6, June 1991.

Calvin, Robert J., "Budgeting Prizes and Profits," *Small Business Reports,* Vol. 18, Issue 7, July 1993.

Chatterjee, Gopalakrishna, Rabikar, and Srinath, "A Communication Response Model for a Mature Industrial Product: Application and Implications," *Journal of Marketing Research,* Vol. 29, Issue 2, May 1992.

Donath, Bob, "Busting Budget Bean Counters," *Marketing News,* Vol. 26, Issue 18, August 31, 1992.

Doyle, Peter, and Saunders, John, "Multiproduct Advertising Budgeting," *Marketing Science,* Vol. 9, Issue 2, Spring 1990.

Falvey, Jack, "The Battle of the Budget," *Sales & Marketing Management,* Vol. 143, Issue 14, November 1991.

Fleming, Mary M.K., and Jizba, Barbara, "Promotion Budgeting and Control in the Fast Food Industry," *International Journal of Advertising,* Vol. 12, Issue 1, 1993.

Frank, Howard A., and Gianakis, Gerasimos A., "Raising the Bridge Using Time Series Forecasting Models," *Public Productiviy & Management Review,* Vol. 14, Issue 2, Winter 1990.

Howell, Keith A., "Lowe's Companies' Statistical Approach to Sales Forecasting," *Corporate Controller,* Vol. 3, Issue 5, May/June 1991.

Hudson, Phillip F., "What Would You Do?" *Bank Marketing,* Vol. 25, Issue 9, September 1993.

Hung, C.L., and West, Douglas C., "Advertising Budgeting Methods in Canada, the UK and the USA," *International Journal of Advertising,* Vol. 10, Issue 3, 1991.

Lamons, Bob, "Let's Demand Enough Money to Do the Job," *Marketing News,* Vol. 27, Issue 8, April 12, 1993.

Lynch, James, E., and Hooley, Graham J., "Increasing Sophistication in Advertising Budget Setting," *Journal of Advertising Research,* Vol. 10, Issue 1, February/March 1990.

O'Neal, Jason, "Budgeting with Trend Projection," *CFO: The Magazine for Senior Financial Executives,* Vol. 7, Issue 8, August 1991.

Pollare, Frank L., "Marketing Public Relations: Surviving the Budgeting Game," *Public Relations Journal,* Vol. 46, Issue 3, March 1990.

Rachlin, Robert, *Total Business Budgeting: A Step-by-Step Guide with Forms,* John Wiley & Sons, Inc., New York, 1991.

Shawkey, Bruce, "Building a High-Performance Budget," *Credit Union Management,* Vol. 15, Issue 8, August 1992.

Symons, Paula, "MCIFs Supply Budget Support," *Credit Union Management,* Vol. 15, Issue 8, August 1992.

Turner, James, "Budgeting Crunch Requires Creative Solutions," *Bank Marketing,* Vol. 23, Issue 9, September 1991.

Turner, James, "Budgeting Crunch Requires Creative Solutions," *Bank Marketing,* Vol. 23, Issue 9, September 1993.

CHAPTER 17

THE RESEARCH AND DEVELOPMENT BUDGET

Maurice I. Zeldman

Emzee Associates

CONTENTS

17.5 MANAGING A BUDGET

(b)   Budget Tracking

Page 17 • 37, replace Exhibit 17.24 with:

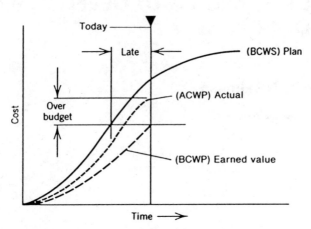

Exhibit 17.24.   Traditional reporting of plan versus actual.

LEASING (New)

Robert Dale Apgood

Canterbury Group

CONTENTS

20A.1 INTRODUCTION. The budgetary process in today's business environment requires a dutiful coordination of a business strategic plan carefully supported by a capital budget (primarily a balance sheet planning tool) and an operating budget (typically an income statement planning tool) (see exhibit 20A.1).

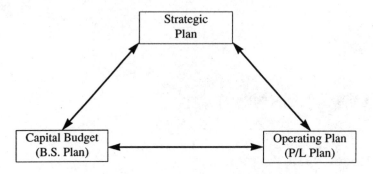

Exhibit 20A.1.   Coordination of planning tools.

Typically top management envisions a strategy and subsequently subordinates are required to project a capital plan (assets, liabilities, and equity) that will enable the company to march toward fulfillment of the strategy vision. Accordingly, a capital budget is prepared, complete with all necessary asset, liability, and equity elements, a process well covered in another chapter of this book. Frequently, however, the company prefers to avoid balance sheet implications by electing to lease assets. Thus, off-balance-sheet financing is selected, the balance sheet impact is minimized, and the operating budget is impacted. To graphically illustrate the financial statement impact, let us examine Exhibit 20A.2.

	OPERATING LEASE		CAPITAL LEASE	
	Balance Sheet	P/L	Balance Sheet	P/L
LESSEE	-0-	Rent expense	Fixed asset	Depreciation expense
			Accumulated depreciation	
			Debt: current long-term	Interest expense
LESSOR	Fixed asset	Depreciation expense		
	Accumulated depreciation		-0-	income
	Debt: current long-term	Interest expense Rental income	(simplest of several possible structures)	

Exhibit 20A.2.   The impact of leasing in financial statements.

From a budgetary viewpoint, it thus becomes evident that leases must be analyzed carefully, in order that the proper budgets become impacted. Occasionally, leasing transactions may be immaterial for a company, but since the mid-1980s, nearly 33% of all property, plant, and equipment acquired by U.S. companies have been acquired through operating and capital leases.[1]

---

[1]Annual statistics available from ELA (Equipment Leasing Association of America), Arlington, Virginia.

Thus the case is made. Budgeting is important and leasing is an increasingly material part thereof.

20A.2   OVERVIEW OF THE LEASING PROCESS.   A typical lease (usually called a single-inventor lease) involves four parties (exhibit 20A.3).

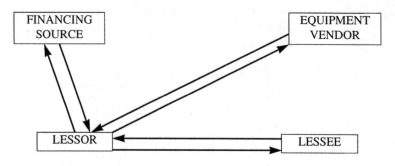

Exhibit 20A.3.   A typical lease.

Simple analysis suggests that, if the lessor retains title to the asset in question, the transaction is a rental or lease. If, however, the lessee eventually ends up with the asset, the lease in question begins to look like some kind of sale from the lessor to the lessee. In budgetary parlance, the transaction is either analyzed as part of the operating budget (if an operating lease) or the capital budget (if a capital lease). Because these two budgets are frequently prepared by different persons, require vastly differing analytical approaches, and dramatically alter balance sheet and income statement presentation, we must become skilled captains of the leasing ship as it sails the financial waters.

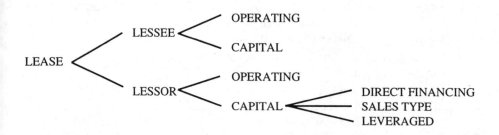

Exhibit 20A.4.   Lease analysis.

Internationally, two different approaches have been taken to properly classify leases on financial statements. The first and simplest approach is observed in the geographical region roughly approximated by southern Europe and is called the "form" approach to leasing. In these countries, if the lease contract stipulates or labels a lease as an operating lease, all analysis is finished. It *is* a rental. Lessor has balance sheet ownership and lessee is a renter. If, in contrast, the lease agreement calls the transaction a capital lease, it *is*. Lessor then accounts for the transaction as a sale and the lessee has balance sheet ownership. How simple! And how consistent! One party is always an owner and the other a nonowner.

But in the United States, as in many other countries, it matter not what a lease is called or labeled. Evidence must be gathered, measurements taken, and then the lease classified as either on- or off-balance sheet for both lessee and lessor. In other words, the substance of a lease dictates its financial statement classification. A short list of countries using each system is displayed in Exhibit 20A.5.

Countries Utilizing Form	Countries Utilizing Substance	Rules of Substance Found in:
France	U.S.	FASB 13, 91, 98, & IAS 17
Italy	U.K.	SSAP 21 & IAS 17
Spain	Canada	CICA 3065 & IAS 17
Portugal	Australia	ASAP 21 & IAS 17
Malta	New Zealand	IAS 17
	Holland	IAS 17
	etc. (approximately 50 additional countries)	IAS 17

Exhibit 20A.5. International lease typology.

As long as both parties to the lease, lessee and lessor, are in the same country, lease treatment will normally be uniform. In the event, however, that a lease becomes bi-national, intriguing cross-border financial results are possible.

Case One:

1. Both the lessee and lessor are in France.
2. The lease document stipulates that the lease is an operating lease—therefore, it is.
3. Lessor assumes balance sheet ownership and is, therefore, entitled to the related income statement deductions for depreciation and interest expenses. Lessor also has balance sheet ramifications.
4. Lessee may not assume balance sheet ownership, but rather must account for the lease as a rental.
5. We have one owner and one nonowner.

	BALANCE SHEET	INCOME STATEMENT
LESSOR	Fixed asset Accumulated depreciation Debt: 　current portion 　long-term portion	Depreciation expense Interest expense Rental income
LESSEE	No impact	Rental expense

Case Two:

1. Lessor is an Italian corporation and lessee is in the United States.
2. The lease document stipulates that the lease is an operating lease. For this lessor, it is.
3. Lessor assumes balance sheet ownership and takes the related income statement deductions for depreciation and interest expenses as well as all balance sheet ramifications.
4. Lessee must follow FASB 13 (U.S. rules). Let us assume that the present value of the minimum lease payments is greater than 90% of the fair value of the leased asset. According to U.S. rules, the lease is a capital lease, the lessee assumes balance sheet ownership also (not necessarily legal ownership), and we have a double-dip lease, or as it is frequently called, a *cross-border tax transfer*.
5. Both lessee and lessor must follow the accounting rules of their countries. Thus, each claims accounting ownership.

	BALANCE SHEET	INCOME STATEMENT

LESSOR	Fixed asset
	Accumulated depreciation
	Debt:
	    current portion
	    long-term portion
		Depreciation expense
		Interest expense
		Rental income

LESSEE	Fixed asset
	Accumulated depreciation
	Debt:
	    current portion
	    long-term portion
		Depreciation expense
		Interest expense

Case Three:

1. Lessor is a Spanish corporation and lessee is in the United States.
2. The lease document stipulates that the lease is a capital lease. For this lessor, it is.
3. Lessor accounts for the lease as a sale. It is no longer on the balance sheet.
4. Lessee must follow FASB 13. Let us assume that the present value of the minimum lease payments is less than 90% of the fair market value of the asset. According to U.S. rules, the lease is an operating lease. The lessee does not have balance sheet ownership and accounts for the transaction as a rental. In this case, neither lessee nor lessor claims balance sheet ownership. It is off the books for each and rightfully so. Lessee and lessor *must* each follow the generally accepted accounting principles of its own country. In the parlance of the leasing community, this is sometimes called a skinny-dip lease, since neither party has balance sheet coverage.

	BALANCE SHEET	INCOME STATEMENT
LESSOR	Nothing. This assumes the asset was sold and the resulting note receivable was also sold.	Income
LESSEE	Nothing	Rental expense

20A.3   POSSIBLE ADVANTAGES OF LEASING.

1. Shifts risk of obsolescence to lessor.
2. Shifts legal ownership and responsibility to lessor.
3. Provides off-balance-sheet financing.
4. Typically paid for from operating budget rather than capital budget.
5. Profitability ratios appear improved.
6. Liquidity ratios appear improved.
7. Solvency ratios appear improved.
8. Tax benefits (depreciation and interest expense) can be shifted to a party better able to utilize them.
9. Lower cash flow up front to obtain asset.
10. Flexibility increases (swaps, upgrades, roll-overs, take-outs, etc.).
11. Inflation hedge (can negotiate longer term and pay with cheaper dollars).
12. Approval can be accelerated.
13. Circumventing capital budget constraints.
14. Delaying sales tax payments (as high as 33% in some European countries).
15. Government reimbursement policies (overhead is frequently a limited or prescribed element for reimbursement; lease payments are not overhead and qualify for reimbursement).
16. Alternative minimum tax (AMT) may dictate no additional purchases.
17. Ownership may be unavailable (satellite usage).
18. Bundling (full-service leases) is facilitated.
19. Excessive usage of equipment by lessee would make ownership unwise.
20. Vendor control (nonperformance of equipment).
21. Finance source diversification.
22. Fewer restriction (bank covenants).
23. Lower cost (lessor may obtain economies of scale and pass through to lessee).

20A.4   POSSIBLE DISADVANTAGES OF LEASING.

1. Opportunity to gain from residual value is shifted to lessor.
2. Balance sheet analysis is hindered, as both asset and liability are disclosed only in footnotes.
3. Capital budgeting decisions are disguised and frequently not analyzed.
4. Tax benefits of ownership: depreciation and interest expense are not normally available to minimize cash flows.

5. Reimbursement policies may be hindered (utilities, for example, are often given a targeted ROA approval figure for rates. If leased, the assets are less and the targeted profitability can be reduced—rates lowered).

6. Higher cost (if lessee is not sophisticated in lease negotiations).

7. Lease versus buy analytical techniques are not universally known and applied.

8. Trends or fads may suggest that leasing is wise when it is only current.

20A.5   TYPES OF LEASE SOURCES.

Lessors

- Financial institutions (banks, savings & loans, finance companies, etc.)
- Captives (vendors and banks)
- Independents

In the United States, independent leasing companies have traditionally held the biggest share of the leasing business.[2] Banks entered the game in a big way in the late 1970s and early 1980s and built large portfolios, many of which were liquidated in the late 1980s and early 1990s as they experienced operating and regulatory difficulties. The current trend in the industry is the awakening and substantial growth of the "vendor" sector, who have discovered that leasing can be a tremendous marketing tool for expansion as well as a profit center.

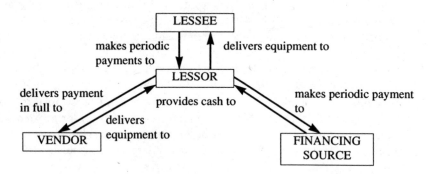

Exhibit 20A.6.   Typical independent lease company transaction (third-party lease).

Many entities have joined the leasing game. They include:

- **Independent leasing companies**—This is the traditional type of lease provider who originally would lease anything to anyone (Exhibit 20A.4). Increased competitive pressure has forced many of these companies to concentrate in niches, such as telecommunications or automobiles. The largest such player is Comdisco, an international participant in Chicago that specialized originally in the used IBM market.

---

[2]ELA statistics.

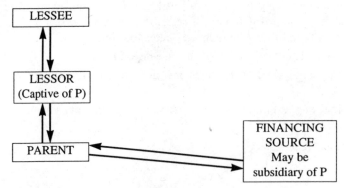

Exhibit 20A.7.   Typical captive lease transaction.

- **Captives**—This is the hot market of the early 1990s. Because they operate under the scrutiny of a parent, they are usually not as nimble and flexible as an independent, but they have tremendous clout becuase of this same parent relationship (exhibit 20A.5). Examples include GECC (General Electric) and ICC (IBM).
- **Brokers**—During the frothy and profitable "go-go" years of the 1980s, many experienced leasing professionals discovered that they could function as financial intermediaries, bringing together the necessary participants, thus functioning as a manager. Brokers come and go, but typically prefer to manage bigger deals, such as jumbo jets and large computer mainframes.
- **Banks**—In the United States, banks entered the leasing game after it was somewhat mature. By way of contrast, banks in Europe and the Middle East were primary developers, and hence currently enjoy a much larger market presence in those geographical regions. U.S. banks dramatically altered their position in the leasing arena during the last few years because of large credit losses and subsequent government tightening of regulations.
- **Insurance companies**—Two approaches have been taken in this industry. Several large firms, such as Metropolitan Life Insurance, formed leasing subsidiaries and aggressively funded deals. Others are content to purchase large individual leases or portfolios on the secondary market, much like the home mortgage market.
- **Finance companies**—Many of these players jumped into the arena, especially in the area of consumer leasing. Because they already were active here, they expanded their horizon to include operating leases and thereby assumed a risk they were not experienced in—residual risk!
- **Pension funds**—Usually these funds serve as a reservoir of lease portfolios and purchased leases from others. Needless to say, many questionable and some worthless paper found its way into the hands of these typically inexperienced participants.
- **Lease pools**—Functioning much like a mutual fund, many lease pools sold "shares" in future expected values to wealthy individuals and companies.

20A.6   LEASE REPORTING.

- FASB 13, 91, 98—Provide criteria for accrual (income statement, balance sheet) reporting.
- IRS Rev. Rul. 55-540, Rev. Proc. 75-21—Provide criteria for tax analysis of a lease.
- IAS 17 (International Accounting Standard 17)—Provides criteria for international lease reporting to the approximately 55 member nations who have adopted it.
- Internal reporting
  a. Lease versus buy
  b. Internal rate of return
  c. Net present value
  d. Breakeven
  e. Pricing
  f. Asset tracking
  g. Accounting
  h. Tax
  i. Billing and collections
  j. Portfolio management.

Software providers have developed an abundance of software application packages to assist in lease analysis and reporting.[3]

(a)   Basic Terminology.   The leasing industry is exceedingly creative, and accordingly a host of synonyms or near-synonyms has been created to describe operating and capital leases. These include the ones listed in exhibit 20A.8.

(b)   Technical Analysis.   Various national and international bodies have labored extensively to codify leasing rules. In the United States, the IRS and FASB have provided mandatory models.

The IRS was the first group in the United States to codify leasing rules, and these still exist. In 1955, Revenue Ruling 55-540 provided initial but very weak "nonguidelines" for lease classifications as either operating or capital. The IRS followed up this initial attempt with an improved but still weak definition of operating and capital in 1975 with Revenue Procedure 75-21. Since then, the IRS has given the lease definition and measurement process little additional attention. Because what it has produced is impractical and insufficient for satisfactory application, the IRS tends to rely upon the subsequent and much superior FASB 13 in its deliberations.

The FASB in 1975 issued FASB 13, which became effective in 1977. This is a much tighter document, which provides definitions and measurements for operating and capital lease classifications.

---

[3]Some of the major software dealers are: Decision Systems, Inc., Minneapolis, Minnesota; SSI, Norcross, Georgia; Better Programs, Denver, Colorado; McCue Systems, Inc., Burlingame, California; The LeMans Group, King of Prussia, Pennsylvania.

Operating Lease Synonyms	Capital Lease Synonyms
operating	capital
real	direct finance
true	finance
rental	installment sales contract
off balance sheet	deferred sales contract
off the books	open-end lease with a bargain purchase option
closed-end	$1.00 purchase option
open-end lease with fair market value purchase option	nominal purchase option
tax	peppercorn (British)
guideline	full payout
non-guideline	full payoff
walk away	sales type
	non-tax
	secured transaction

Exhibit 20A.8.   Basic terminology to describe operating and capital leases.

(c)   FASB 13.   FASB 13 contains the four criteria that must be observed if a lease is to be classified as a capital lease.

(i)   Four Tests of Substance.

1. Will title pass from lessor to lessee?
2. Does the lease contain a bargain purchase option?
3. Is the lease life greater than or equal to 75% of the economic life?
4. Is the present value of the minimum lease payments greater than or equal to 90% of the fair market value of the equipment?

If the answer to any of these questions is affirmative, the lease is a capital lease. If all four are negative, the lease is an operating lease.

Internationally, all of the previously mentioned lease codification numbers (CICA 3065 in Canada, FASB 13 in the United States, SSAP 21 in England, etc.) are substantially identical and are also substantially identical to IAS 17, issued by the International Accounting Standards Board in London. In other words, once the intricacies of FASB 13 are mastered, all others are virtually identical.

Therefore, these four tests must be carefully examined and mastered if the financial statements are to be properly stated *and* if the budgeting classifications of operating and capital assets are to be proper. An operating lease will be included in the operating "budget" and is usually approved by a department head. A capital lease, on the other hand, is in the capital budget and is typically approved by someone at a higher corporate level.

(ii)   Analysis of the Four Tests.   The first test is simple to control. If an operating lease is desired, do not provide for the transfer of title in the lease document. Simply state that the lease is a closed-end lease or a walk-away lease (i.e., no purchase

option is available to the lessee). Conversely, if a capital lease is desired, stipulate how and when title will pass (i.e., after 24 payments, after 60 months, etc.).

The second test is equally easy to control. If an operating lease is desired, avoid the inclusion of a bargain purchase option (B.P.O.) in the lease agreement. If the parties to the lease desire a capital lease, a B.P.O provision automatically qualifies the lease as a purchase.

The third test is quite easy to control once one term is mastered—*economic life.* As used in the leasing industry, and in contrast to accounting and tax usage, life of an asset in its "economic" sense is defined as the expected useful life. Fully deciphered, FASB and the leasing industry define *economic life* as the length of time the asset has usefulness to multiple, subsequent users, not just the present user. Thus, economic life assumes a measure much longer than book life and considerably longer than tax life—a long, long life. Thus, cars usually are given an economic life of 10 to 15 years, mainframe computers 12 to 15 years, and ordinary desks and chairs a life of 15 to 20. The budget analyst who is trying to convert a lease into a capital variety is probably wise not to try to qualify it with this third test. Lease lives are virtually always much less than 75% of the economic life. This third test will normally result in a rental situation.

Understanding and manipulating (not meant in its derogatory connotation) the budgetary journey of a lease from operating to capital usually involves a very mundane control of the fourth test—the present value of cash flows. This can easily be the point of departure where the budget novice errs, concluding that a lease is operating when in fact it should be capital and vice versa. In short, the forecasted balance sheet and income statement are in danger of being misbudgeted and malforecasted.

To shorten the fourth test, we observe the technical language of FASB 13.

$$(PV)(MLP's) \geq (90\%)(FMV)$$

If the present value of the minimum lease payments is greater than or equal to 90% of the FMV, a capital lease exists. Of course, the result is an operating lease if the 90% line of demarcation is not reached Now to understand the implications of the formula.

(iii) Present Value—How?   FASB 13 dictates the alternative discounting rates to be utilized by the lessor and lessee.

Discount Rate to Be Utilized by Lessor	Lower of Discount Rate to Be Utilized by Lessee
The lessor must present-value the cash flows using the implicit rate in the lease.	The lessee must use the lower of: 1. The lessor's implicit rate in the lease, if known by the lessee. or 2. The incremental borrowing rate of the lessee.

Let us examine why FASB directed that the implicit rate is the only acceptable rate for the lessor. In order to establish its logic, let us pictorially examine the cash flows of the lessor in a leasing transaction (see Exhibits 20A.9 and 20A.10).

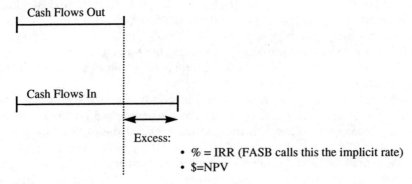

Exhibit 20A.9.

Lessor

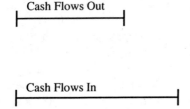

Exhibit 20A.10.

Possible cash flows out for the lessor include:

1. Equipment cost (broadly defined as historical cost of the equipment plus freight-in, installation, debugging, etc.).
2. Initial direct costs (referred to in FASB 13 and FASB 91 as I.D.C.s)
   A. Commissions paid by lessor to sales representative to obtain lease
   B. Lawyers' fees paid by lessor to structure document
   C. Credit investigation fees paid by lessor to ascertain creditworthiness of lessee
   D. Other costs.

Possible cash flows in for the lessor include:

1. Initial (at inception date of lease)
   A. Advance payments
   B. Refundable fees
   C. Nonrefundable fees.
2. Periodic (typically occur monthly in U.S. lease transactions but frequently quarterly or semiannually in European deals).

3. Terminal (at the end of the lease terrn)
   A. Fees (nonrefundable fees, pick-up fees, refurbishing fees, etc.)
   B. Sale (could either be to the lessee or to a third party)
   C. Re-lease (could either be to the lessee or to a third party)
   D. Lessee-guaranteed residual value (which automatically makes the lease a capital lease, as all risk has effectively been removed for the lessor)
   E. Third-party residual insurance (the lessor could buy an insurance policy at lease inception date providing for a stipulated terminal value).

Now let us quickly cast our gaze again at the top of Exhibit 20A.10, keeping in mind that we are examining it from the viewpoint of the lessor. It becomes clear that the lessor knows with precision each and every cash flow assumption (interpret this to mean budget or forecast) in the exhibit. Thus, the lessor can indeed calculate the implicit rate in the lease because the lessor knows all the data.

Next, let us remove our lessor hat and replace it with that of the lessee—think like a lessee. Look again at Exhibit 20A.10. The lessee rarely knows the equipment cost, never knows the commissions paid, the lawyers' fees, the credit investigation charges, and so on. In other words, the lessee does not know all cash flows out. Likewise, the lessee does not know all cash flows in. Some budgeted (estimated) flows in are known, such as the initial and the periodic flows, but the lessee would only know the terminal budgeted flows if the lessee holds a purchase or renewal option. In conclusion, the lessee would virtually never know all cash flows forecasted in a lease transaction. Thus, lessee could not possibly calculate the implicit rate inherent in the lease. The only other way for the lessee to know (notice FASB 13 did not use the words, "estimate the implicit rate"—it says "know it") the implicit rate would be to ask the lessor for it. Because the implicit rate is also the profitability rate inherent in the lease transaction, no lessor would or could divulge such detail to an outside party. In other words, the lessee normally cannot know the implicit rate. This brings us to the alternative discount rate posited by FASB for use by the lessee—the incremental, pretax, installment, secured, co-terminus borrowing rate— what rate would the lessee have to pay to borrow a like sum for a like period for a like transaction? A strong lessee might, therefore, select prime, whereas a weaker lessee would add several percentage points to the rate.

Lessor and lessee will each present value the budgeted cash flows, but each will use a different rate. If each uses a different rate, one set of cash flows could be above the magic 90% and the other below. Conclusion: it is possible, and indeed desirable, that the sophisticated lessor and lessee may structure the budgeted lease so that each gets the desired result, which could be:

1. Single-dip lease—on one set of books only
2. Double-dip lease—on both sets of books
3. Skinny dip lease—on neither set of books.

Enough of rates. Let's move on to MLPs, the second element in the formula of test number four.

(d) Minimum Lease Payments. FASB 13 directs lessors and lessees to present-value the minimum lease payments (MLPs). MLPs are not all but just some of the cash flows in the lease—the flows that can be predicted or budgeted with certainty.

LESSOR	LESSEE
1. Periodic payment in lease (usually monthly payment)	1. Periodic payment in lease (usually monthly payment)
2. Guaranteed residual payment	2. Lessee-guaranteed residual payments
3. Nonrenewal penalties	3. Nonrenewal penalties
4. *BUT* Fees, per FASB 91, are to be capitalized by lessor and amortized over the lease life, thus impacting future budget periods	4. Fees
5. Bargain purchase option	5. Bargain purchase option
6. *But not* executory costs	6. *But not* executory costs
7. Third-party residual insurance on the terminal value of the equipment	

Let's take a brief detour to discuss executory costs, after which we'll return to MLPs. Executory costs are defined in FASB 13 and 91 as cash flows out—operating costs paid by the lessee once a lease is in place. A logical way to picture these appears in Exhibit 20A.11.

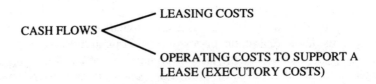

CASH FLOWS ⟨ LEASING COSTS

OPERATING COSTS TO SUPPORT A
LEASE (EXECUTORY COSTS)

Exhibit 20A.11. Executory costs.

NET LEASE	FULL SERVICE LEASE OR BUNDLED LEASE
The lease pays only a: 1. Low net monthly payment (assume $500) PLUS 2. Executory (operating) costs (assume $300 per month)	The lessee pays a higher monthly payment to lessor who, in turn, pays the executory costs. New monthly payment would be approximately $500 + $300 = $800.

Exhibit 20A.12. Lessee executory costs.

Now assume:

$$(PV)(\$500) = 92\% \text{ of FV} = \text{capital lease}$$

Lessee may not desire a budgeted capital transaction, so the two parties negotiate a bundled lease resulting in the $800 monthly budgeted payment being allocated as shown in Exhibit 20A.13.

PAYMENT $800 — $450 TO MLP

$350 TO BUNDLED SERVICES

Exhibit 20A.13.   Bundled lease.

Thus, the (PV)($450) < 90% FMV and the lessee gets an operating lease. Real-world evidence of this exists in the normal lease proposals of Xerox, IBM, and many other companies, wherein they push bundling. They want to provide a machine plus supplies, maintenance, insurance, training, and any other product and/or services.

If the lessee desires a budgeted capital lease, the agreement can bundle more cash flow into the monthly payment. If, however, the capital budget is all used up, bundle a lease so that less of the cash flow is attributed to the monthly payment and an operating lease is created.

Now let's return from our detour to the MLP discussion. Notice that FASB directed that executory costs not be included in the MLP to be present-valued. Also, notice that the minimum lease payments listed under lessor and lessee are *not* the same.

The result? If different budgeted cash flows are present-valued, it is possible to:

1. Single-dip a lease
2. Double-dip a lease
3. Skinny-dip a lease.

(e)   The 90 Percent Rule.   In all countries of the world that follow the rules of substance (not form countries), there is general agreement on the 90% rule. However, the lessee and lessor each must measure according to "known" information. Thus, the lessor and lessee end up with different comparison bases (90% of the fair market value).

Lessor	Lessee
90% of "the" FMV	90% of "a" FMV

Because the exact cost of the equipment is known to the lessor, the lessor can indeed make this calculation. The lessee, however, normally will not "know with precision" the FMV. Thus, an estimate must suffice. Conceptually, this means that the lessee will rely upon one of the following for the fair market value:

1. Written bid
2. Telephone quotation
3. Newspaper advertisement
4. Price list—wholesale
5. Price list—retail
6. Estimated cost
7. Other.

Conclusion: Rarely would the lessor and the lessee take 90% of the same cost.

(f) Retrospect.   Once again, let us examine the fourth test of substance.

$$(PV)(\text{Minimum Lease Payments}) \geq 90\% \text{ of the Fair Market Value}$$

As we have seen, lessor and lessee will utilize different variables for three of the four test components. It is not only possible but probable that each can control the variables to obtain the desired type of lease and thereby shift impact from the operating budget to the capital budget or vice versa.

20A.7   LEASE VERSUS PURCHASE ANALYSIS.   Lease versus purchase analysis begins with the assumption that the investment analysis (capital budgeting) decision has been made in favor of acquiring a piece of equipment. The next step requires a financing decision—lease versus purchase analysis.

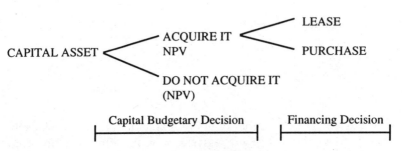

Exhibit 20A.14.   Lease versus purchase analysis.

Mega Corp. recently decided to obtain a computer with a retail value of $400,000. The company can either obtain a loan and purchase the computer, or it can be leased. Mega Corp. is in the 40% tax bracket.

(a) Relevant Inforrnation for Purchase Alternative.   A bank loan must be obtained for the purchase price of $400,000 less a down payment of $100,000. The balance ($300,000) is to be financed over 36 months with monthly payments in arrears of $9,680, an implicit borrowing rate of about 10%. Sales tax is 6% and will be paid at the time of purchase. The bank requires a loan origination fee of 2% of the loan proceeds. Each monthly payment is composed of both principal and interest, the latter being tax deductible as follows:

Year 1	$25,939
Year 2	$16,492
Year 3	$ 6,055

Depreciation expense on the computer will be straight line for book purposes and Modified Accelerated Cost Recovery System (MACRS) with a five-year life for tax. The sales tax of $24,000 will be capitalized as part of the computer's depreciable base.

(b)   Depreciation Calculation.

Weighted Average Aftertax Cost of Capital of 12%.

Equipment cost	$400,000
Sales tax	24,000
Depreciable basis	$424,000

Year 1	$84,800	(20%)(424,000)
Year 2	135,680	(32%)(424,000)
Year 3	81,408	(19.2%)(424,000)
Year 4	48,760	(11.5%)(424,000)
Year 5	48,760	(11.5%)(424,000)
Year 6	24,592	(5.8%)(424,000)
	$424,000	

Operating costs (executory cost):

1. Repairs and maintenance = $1,000 per month for 72 months
2. Insurance = $400 per month for 72 months
3. Supplies = $700 per month for 72 months

Preset Value Factors:

Type of Flow	Rate	N	Factor
PV annuity	.83%	36 months	31.0093
PV annuity	1%	72 months	51.1504
PV annuity	1%	70 months	50.1685
PV annuity	.83%	72 months	54.0375
PV of 1	12%	3 years	0.7118
PV of 1	12%	2 years	0.7972
PV of 1	12%	1 year	0.8929
PV of 1	12%	4 years	0.6355
PV of 1	12%	5 years	0.5674
PV of 1	12%	6 years	0.5066

HP 12 C keystrokes for loan amortization:

300,000 CHS PV

g end
9,680 PMT
10 g 12 ÷
0 n

12 f amort	25,939
X ⋛ Y	90,221
RCL PV	209,779
12 f amort	16,492
X ⋛ Y	99,668
RCL PV	110,111
12 f amort	6,055
X ⋛ Y	110,105
RCL PV	7 (Rounding error)

(c) Leasing Information.   The lease would be for six years with monthly payments of $8,250 in advance. The first and last two payments are due at the lease inception date. A lease origination fee of $4,000 must be paid in advance. The lease contains a fair market value purchase option, but Mega Corp. does not plan on exercising the option.

Operating costs (executory costs) are:

1. Use tax of 6% on each monthly payment = $495
2. Insurance = $425 per month
3. Repairs and maintenance = $1,000 per month
4. Supplies = $600 per month.

Present Value of Purchase Alternative

	Cash Flow	x PV Factor	x Tax Factor	= Amount
Initial flows:				
Down payment	$100,000	1	N/A	$100,000
Sales tax	24,000	1	N/A	24,000
	6,000	1	1-0.4	3,600
Periodic flows:	9,680	31.0	N/A	300,080
Terminal flows:				
Repairs and				
maintenance	1,000	54.04	1-0.4	32,424
Insurance	400	54.04	1-0.4	12,970
Supplies	700	54.04	1-0.4	22,697

Tax shielded by:
  Interest expense   (16,247)
  Depreciation
    expense   (125,176)
Net present value of aftertax cash flows to purchase $354,348

Present Value of Leasing Alternative

	Cash Flow	x PV Factor	x Tax Factor	= Amount
Initial flows:				
Advance payments (2)	$16,500	1	1-0.4	$9,900
	4,000	1	1-0.4	2,400
Periodic flows:				
Monthly payments (70)	8,250	50.17	1-0.4	248,342
Terminal flows:				
Use tax in advance (2)	990	1	1-0.4	594
Use tax	495	50.17	1-0.4	14,900
Insurance	425	50.17	1-0.4	12,793
Repairs and maintenance	1000	50.17	1-0.4	30,102
Supplies	600	50.17	1-0.4	18,061
Net present value of aftertax cash flows to lease				$310,001

Calculation of Tax Shielded by Interest Expense:

Year	Interest Expense	PV Factor	Tax Factor	Income Tax Shielded
1	$25,939	0.8929	0.4	$9,264
2	16,492	0.7972	0.4	5,259
3	6,055	0.7118	0.4	1,724
	$48,486			$16,247

Calculation of Tax Shielded by Depreciation Expense

Year	Interest Expense	PV Factor	Tax Factor	Income Tax Shielded
1	$84,800	0.8929	0.4	$30,287
2	135,680	0.7972	0.4	43,266
3	81,408	0.7118	0.4	23,178
4	48,760	0.6355	0.4	12,395
5	48,760	0.5674	0.4	11,067
6	24,592	0.5066	0.4	4,983
	$424,000			$125,176

20A.8   FASB 13 CASE ILLUSTRATION.

Lease provisions
Lease term: 60 months
List price of equipment: $140,000
Discount to lessor from vendor: $14,000
First and last two payments due at inception date
Nonrenewal penalty: $1,500
Estimated residual value: $19,000
Monthly payment, net of executory costs: $2,600.

(a)   Lessor Solution.

Step 1: Calculation of Implicit Rate

Keystrokes	Display	Explanation
f REG	0.00	Clears all registers
118,200 CHS g CFo	118,200	Enters initial cash flow
2,600 g CFj	2,600	Enters first cash flow
57 g Nj	57.00	Enters number of times first flow occurs
0 g CFj	0.00	Enters second cash flow
2 g Nj	2.00	Enters number of times second flow occurs
20,500 g CFj	20,500	Enters third cash flow
f IRR	1.16	Answer (the calculated monthly yield)
12X	13.94	IRR (the implicit rate)

Step 2: PV of MLPs

Keystrokes	Display	Explanation
f REG	0.00	Clears all registers
1.16 i	1.16	Enters monthly discount rate
7,800 g CFo	7,800.00	Enters initial cash flow
2,600 g CFj	2,600.00	Enters first cash flow
57 g Nj	57.00	Enters number of times first flow occurs
0 g CFj	0.00	Enters second cash flow
2 g Nj	2.00	Enters number of times second flow occurs
1,500 g CFj	1,500.00	Enters third cash flow
f NPV	116,540.57	Answer (the calculated net present value)

Step 3: Calculation of a Comparison Base

$126,000
x ____0.9
$113,400

Conclusion: Capital lease, because the PV of the MLPs is more than 90% of the FMV.

(b)   Lessee Solution.

Step 1: PV of MLPs

Keystrokes	Display	Explanation
f REG	0.00	Clears all registers
10 g 12 ÷	0.83	Enters monthly discount rate
7,800 g CFo	7,800	Enters initial cash flow
2,600 g CFj	2,600	Enters first cash flow
57 g Nj	57.00	Enters number of times first flow occurs
0 g CFj	0.00	Enters second cash flow
2 g Nj	2.00	Enters number of times second flow occurs
1,500 g CFj	1,500	Enters third cash flow
f NPV	126,301.28	Answer (the calculated present value)

Step 2: Calculation of a Comparison Base

$$\begin{array}{r} \$140,000 \\ \underline{\times \qquad 0.9} \\ \$126,000 \end{array}$$

Conclusion: Capital lease, because the PV of the MLPs is more than 90% of the FMV.

(c)   Conclusion.   For the lessor, the lease would be classified as a capital lease because (PV)(MLP) ≥ (90%)(FMV). But for the lessee, the lease could be either operating or capital, depending on the choice of the PV rate. If the lease is being analyzed near the end of the year and if the lessee has extra cash available in the operating budget, an operating lease could be structured, keeping the deal off the books. If, however, the lessee has cash left in the capital budget, a direct finance lease could be structured, thereby putting the equipment on the books.

It becomes imperative that budget experts, both operating and capital, understand the principles dictated by FASB 13 in order to optimize plans and results.

20A.9   NEGOTIATION OF LEASES.   How do you negotiate a lease? Many factors must be considered, including, but not limited to:

1. Number of periodic payments
2. Number of advance payments
3. Stub payments (partial initial payments)
4. Nonrenewal penalties
5. Lease origination fees
6. Contingent payments
7. Excess usage or "beat up" fees
8. Deposits
9. Step up, step down, skip payment provisions
10. COLA or other escalation provisions
11. Tax indemnifications

12. Equipment subleasing rights
13. Usage restrictions
14. Late payment penalties
15. Leasehold improvement ownership rights
16. Lease assignment rights
17. Lessor subrogation rights
18. Executory cost provisions (insurance, supplies, repairs, taxes, etc.)
19. Warranties on equipment by vendor and/or lessor
20. Rollovers, upgrades, early outs, swaps
21. Renewal options
22. Purchase options
23. Residual value insurance
24. Equipment inspection provisions
25. Equipment maintenance provisions.

20A.10   SELECTING A LESSOR.   Lessor selection demands that the lessee consider:

- Financial condition of leasing company
- Flexibility
- Services offered
- Rate commitment
- Turnaround time
- Prior experience with similar equipment
- Geographic presence
- Financing sources
- Ultimate disposition of lease paper.

20A.11   LEASE ANALYSIS TECHNIQUES.   There are many types of returns which may be calculated for any lease transaction. These measures of performance are usually stated in some form of return on investment. Typical returns would be stated as the internal rate of return for a particular transaction or the "return" on a portfolio. The return on a portfolio would be some type of weighted average calculation. However, all quoted returns are based on cash flows, or, in other words, when cash changes hands. Some of the different titles for types of returns would be:

- Internal Rate of Return
- External Rate of Return
- Modified Rate of Return
- Street Rate or Stream Rate
- Return on Assets
- Return on Equity
- Average Return on Assets
- Yield

Because so many different names may be used, it would be easier to take a particular transaction and view the different types of return calculations from the lessee and lessor perspectives. For this example, the following assumptions will be utilized in developing different yield calculations:

1. Lease term: Four years with the first rental payment due at the end of the first year of the lease. For tax purposes, the lease is considered a true or guideline lease; that is, the lessor will be entitled to the tax benefits of tax depreciation, and the lessee will be entitled to expense the full amount of the payments made to the lessor.

2. At the conclusion of the lease term, the lessee will have the option of purchasing the equipment for its then fair market value, renewing the lease for the equipment at its then fair market value, or returning the equipment to the lessor and having no further involvement with the particular piece of equipment.

3. The lessor is a calendar year taxpayer in the 35% tax bracket.

4. The annual rental shall be $60,000 and the inception date of the lease transaction is December 31.

5. The purchase price or fair market value of the equipment is $200,000.

6. The expected fair market value of the equipment at the end of the lease term is $30,000, as estimated by the lessor at the inception of the lease arrangement.

7. The lessor will require a $5,000 refundable security deposit from the lessee. This amount will be held by the lessor throughout the term of the lease and returned to the lessee at the end of the lease term if there is no reason to use it for default reasons. The lessor will not pay the lessee any monies for the use of these funds.

8. A $ 1,000 nonrefundable commitment fee is to be received by the lessor from the lessee.

9. A $2,500 brokerage fee is to be paid by the lessor to a third party as compensation for its bringing this transaction to the lessor.

10. General and administrative costs have been allocated to the lease along with the initial direct costs of $4,000. First-year general and administrative costs are $3,000 and have a 5% inflation factor built in.

11. Tax benefits are assumed to result fully in tax savings.

The "interest" cost to the lessee is the first type of yield calculation to be performed. The lessee "cost" is calculated because a lease transaction does not contain a stated interest rate or cost of money, as a lease is a usage transaction and not a money-financing transaction. The lessor is providing the use of equipment and not the lending of money to the lessee to be used for whatever purpose it desires.

From the lessee's perspective, it is gaining the use of $200,000 of equipment for four years and at the end of four years it has a number of options which may be exercised at its discretion. If the lessee returns the equipment to the lessor at the end of the initial lease term, then it would have the use of $200,000 for four years at a cost of $60,000, payments in arrears for the four-year period. The "interest" cost of money would be 7.71 percent. If the lessee were to purchase the equipment at the end of the four-year term for the lessor's estimated fair market value of $30,000, the "interest" cost of money would be 12.29%. If the lessee were to renew the equipment lease at the end of the four-year term, it would not be possible to calculate an "interest" cost of money to the lessor, because the terms of the renewal are not yet known, even if the renewal amount of $30,000 were to be known.

Both the 7.71% and 12.29% calculations are pretax. From the perspective of the lessee, any aftertax calculations would be based on a number of assumptions and are really not relevant to an understanding of this transaction.

The remainder of the calculations in this chapter are from the lessor perspective and are done from both a pretax and aftertax perspective. The calculations are numerous and it can readily be seen why confusion often reigns when trying to compare yields in lease transactions. One must understand what elements of cash flow are included when arriving at a particular stated yield and whether the calculation is pretax or aftertax. To fully understand aftertax calculations, one must also understand the leverage or gearing of the lessor and whether the transactions have been funded on a pooled or match-funded basis, the pretax cost of debt to the lessor, and whether the rate is fixed throughout the transaction or is adjusted at times throughout the lease term in accordance with some borrowing agreement in place for the lessor. The corporate tax rate and the timing of when taxes are remitted enter into a fine tuning of any calculation, and the desired return on equity contributed funds plays perhaps the most important role of all these variables.

Pretax lessor calculations would be as follows:

1. *Stream or street rate.* This calculation only takes into account the cost of the equipment to the lessor and any noncancelable payment amounts. Because the residual amount is anticipated but not absolutely known (unknown to the lessee), it would be the same as making a $200,000 investment and receiving $60,000 per year in arrears for the use of this invested amount. This would be a return of 7.71% and compares with the same amount as calculated by the lessee previously.

2. *Stream rate including residual.* This calculation includes the expected, but unguaranteed, residual amount of $30,000. When the residual is included in the calculation, then the lessor yield would be 12.29% and would be equivalent to the similar calculation of the lessee as performed previously.

3. *Pretax payback.* Both the stream rate and stream rate with residual calculations would indicate a payback period of 3.33 years. This does not take into account any adjustment for the time value of money. A time-adjusted payback period could be calculated if one were to assume some hurdle rate or cost of funds to the lessor. For purposes of this chapter, this calculation is not performed, but could be readily accomplished if some hurdle rate were to be brought into focus.

4. *An all-inclusive pretax return on asset yield.* This amount would include all of the pretax cash flows and would be based on when the cash is expected to change hands. This would take into account all known and expected cash flows to be received by the lessor, but does not take into account the tax benefits to be received and utilized by the lessor. In our example, the cash flows would occur as follows:

Initial or inception:

($200,000)	Equipment cost
(2,500)	Brokerage fee
(4,000)	Initial direct costs
1,000	Nonrefundable fee
5,000	Refundable security deposit
($200,500)	Net outflow at inception

During the term of the transaction:

Three payments of $60,000 per year

At termination:

$60,000	Final payment amount
30,000	Purchase option amount
(5,000)	Security deposit refund
$85,000	Net termination inflow

When taking into account all of these cash flows and the timing of when they would occur, the yield to the lessor is 11.47%. This is close to the 12.29% amount previously calculated, but includes all cash flows. As must be noted, this is a lower value than the stream rate including the residual.

5. *Net, pretax yield.* This calculation takes into account all of the cash flows as shown in item 4 with the addition of the general and administrative costs. The following illustration shows the timing of the cash flows and results in a pretax yield to the lessor of 9.25%. The 9.25% value is calculated by determining the internal rate of return for the cash flow amounts for each year of the transaction.

	0	1	2	3	4
Rental payments	0	60,000	60,000	60,000	60,000
Commitment fee	1,000				
Initial direct costs	(4,000)	0	0	0	0
Brokerage fee	(2,500)				
G&A	0	(3,000)	(3,150)	(3,308)	(3,473)
Residual	0	0	0	0	30,000
Security deposit	(5,000)	0	0	0	(5,000)
Deduct: cost of equipment	(200,000)	0	0	0	0
TOTAL	(200,500)	57,000	56,850	56,692	81,527

f IRR = 9.25

6. *Net, aftertax yield.* This calculation takes into account the cash flows included in the previous calculations and then includes the impact of recovering the lessor's investment through tax depreciation. It is seen that this net, aftertax yield is 7.00%. Some analysts will arrive at the aftertax yield by multiplying the pretax yield of 9.25% by the reciprocal of the tax rate, or 65%. If this were done (9.25 times 0.65), the resultant yield would be 6.01%. As can be seen when calculating the internal rate of return for the final cash flows, the yield is 7.00%. The difference is due to the timing of the cash flows, which is not taken into account when performing the 6.01% calculation.

	0	1	2	3	4
Rental payments	0	60,000	60,000	60,000	60,000
Commitment fee	1,000	0	0	0	0
Initial direct costs	(4,000)	0	0	0	0
Brokerage fee	(2,500)	0	0	0	0
G&A	0	(3,000)	(3,150)	(3,308)	(3,473)
Depreciation	(40,000)	(64,000)	(38,400)	(23,040)	(34,560)
Residual	0	0	0	0	30,000
Pretax income	(45,500)	(7,000)	18,450	33,652	51,967
Taxes @ 35%	15,925	2,450	(6,458)	(11,778)	(18,188)
A-T income	(29,575)	(4,550)	11,993	21,874	33,779
Add: depreciation	40,000	64,000	38,400	23,040	34,560
Security deposit	5,000	0	0	0	0
Deduct: cost of equipment	(200,000)	0	0	0	0
TOTAL	(184,575)	59,450	50,393	44,914	63,339

7. *Return on equity.* This final calculation is found by making assumptions as to the method of funding employed by the lessor which, in this example, assumes that the lessor wishes the lease. Also, the leverage employed by the lessor is 80% debt and 20% equity. The pretax interest cost on borrowed funds is 9% and the tax rate of the lessor throughout the life of the transaction will be 35%. The return on equity for the lessor based on the cash flows calculated in 6 and adjusted for the cost of debt and including the repayment of borrowed funds is 11.60%. This amount is found by deducting the aftertax cost of debt from the aftertax cost of capital as calculated in 6.00 or 7.00%. The aftertax cost of debt to the lessor is found by multiplying the pretax cost of debt times the quantity (one minus the tax rate or 0.65) times the 0.8 debt leverage factor. This is found to be 4.68%.

When this amount is deducted from aftertax cost of capital of 7.00%, the cost of equity is determined to be 2.32%. When this is divided by the 0.2 equity leverage factor, the return on equity to the lessor is determined as 11.60%.

Net Aftertax Cash Flows

0	1	2	3	4
(184,575)	59,450	50,393	44,914	63,339

80% Debt = 147,660
20% Equity = 36,915

Year One

147,660 x 0.09 = 13,289 x 0.65 =   8,638 A-T Return on Debt
36,915 x 11.60 =   4,282 A-T Return on Equity
                                                            12,920
.8 x 9(.65) = 4.68   (59,450) CF
.2 x 11.60 = 2.32   46,530
         7.00   x .8
                                                            37,224 Debt
                                                             9,306 Equity

Year Two

147,660 - 37,224 = 110,436 x 0.09 = 9.939 x 0.65 =   6,461 A-T Return on Debt
36,915 - 9,306 = 27,609 x 0.1160 =   3,203 A-T Return on Equity
                                                             9,664
                                                            (50,393) CF
                                                            40,729
                                                             x .8
                                                            32,583 Debt
                                                             8,146 Equity

Year Three

110,436 - 32,583 = 77,853 x 0.09 = 7,007 x 0.65 =   4,554 A-T ROD
27,609 - 8,246 = 19,463 x 0.1160 =   2,258 A-T ROE
                                                             6,812
                                                            (44,914) CF
                                                            38,102
                                                             x .8
                                                            30,482 Debt
                                                             7,620 Equity

Year Four

77,853 - 30,482 = 47,371 x 0.09 = 4,263 x 0.65 =   2,771 ROD
         [x]
19,463 - 7,620 = 11,843 x 0.1160 =   1,374 ROE
         [y]   4,145
                                                            (63,339) CF
                                                            59,194
                                                             x .8

[x] 16 Δ due to rounding.   [x] 47,355 Debt
[y] 4 Δ due to rounding.   [y] 11,839 Equity

20A.12   LEASE FORM.

AGREEMENT NO. _____

EQUIPMENT LEASE

LESSOR: _____   LESSEE: _____

_____   _____
(STREET ADDRESS)   (STREET ADDRESS)

_____   _____
(CITY, STATE, AND ZIP)   (CITY, STATE, AND ZIP)

Description of Leased Equipment

NEW/USED   QUANTITY   MAKE and DESCRIPTION   SERIAL NO.

EQUIPMENT LOCATION: ☐ SAME AS ABOVE   ☐ OTHER: (address) _____

LEASE PAYMENT TERMS

MONTHS	AMOUNTS
TOTAL LEASE TERM # _____ MONTHS	MONTHLY RENTAL AMOUNT: _____
	PLUS USE TAX, IF ANY
ADVANCE RENTALS PAID # _____ MONTHS	TOTAL RENTALS PAID IN ADVANCE: _____
	RENTAL x # PAID

TERMS AND CONDITIONS OF LEASE

LESSEE HEREBY WARRANTS AND REPRESENTS THAT THE EQUIPMENT WILL BE USED FOR BUSINESS PURPOSES, AND NOT FOR PERSONAL, FAMILY, HOUSEHOLD, OR AGRICULTURAL PURPOSES. LESSEE ACKNOWLEDGES THAT LESSOR AND ITS ASSIGNS HAVE RELIED UPON THIS REPRESENTATION IN ENTERING INTO THIS LEASE.

1. LESSEE ACKNOWLEDGES THAT LESSOR IS NOT THE MANUFACTURER OF THE EQUIPMENT, NOR MANUFACTURER'S AGENT AND LESSEE REPRESENTS THAT LESSEE HAS SELECTED THE EQUIPMENT LEASED HEREUNDER BASED UPON LESSEE'S JUDGMENT

(Continued on next pages.)

THE UNDERSIGNED AGREE TO ALL THE TERMS AND CONDITIONS SET FORTH ABOVE AND ON THE REVERSE SIDE HEREOF, AND IN WITNESS

WHEREOF, HEREBY EXECUTES THIS LEASE AND CERTIFIES THAT THE UNDERSIGNED IS DULY AUTHORIZED TO EXECUTE SAME, ON BEHALF OF OR AS THE LESSEE AND THAT HE HAS RECEIVED AN EXECUTED COPY OF THIS LEASE.

Executed this _____ day of _____, 19__.

LESSOR: _____   LESSEE: _____

By: _____   BY: _____
                                                          TITLE

TITLE: _____   BY: _____
                                                          TITLE

PRIOR TO HAVING REQUESTED THE LEASE. THE EQUIPMENT LEASED HEREUNDER IS OF A DESIGN, SIZE, FITNESS, AND CAPACITY SELECTED BY LESSEE AND LESSEE IS SATISFIED THAT THE SAME IS SUITABLE AND FIT FOR ITS INTENDED PURPOSES. LESSEE FURTHER AGREES THAT <u>LESSOR HAS MADE AND MAKES NO REPRESENTATIONS OR WARRANTIES OF WHATSOEVER NATURE, DIRECTLY OR INDIRECTLY, EXPRESSED OR IMPLIED, INCLUDING BUT NOT LIMITED TO ANY REPRESENTATIONS OR WARRANTIES WITH RESPECT TO SUITABILITY, DURABILITY, FITNESS FOR USE AND MERCHANTABILITY OF ANY SUCH EQUIPMENT, THE PURPOSES AND USES OF THE LESSEE, OR OTHERWISE.</u> LESSEE SPECIFICALLY WAIVES ALL RIGHTS TO MAKE CLAIM AGAINST LESSOR HEREIN FOR BREACH OF ANY WARRANTY OF ANY KIND WHATSOEVER. LESSOR HEREBY PASSES TO LESSEE ALL WARRANTIES, IF ANY, RECEIVED BY LESSOR BY VIRTUE OF ITS OWNERSHIP OF THE EQUIPMENT. LESSOR SHALL NOT BE LIABLE TO LESSEE FOR ANY LOSS, DAMAGE, OR EXPENSE OF ANY KIND OR NATURE CAUSED DIRECTLY OR INDIRECTLY BY ANY EQUIPMENT LEASED HEREUNDER FOR THE USE OR MAINTENANCE THEREOF, OR FOR THE FAILURE OF OPERATIONS THEREOF, OR BY ANY INTERRUPTION OF SERVICE OR LOSS OF USE THEREOF OR FOR ANY LOSS OF BUSINESS OR ANY OTHER DAMAGE WHATSOEVER AND HOWSOEVER CAUSED. NO DEFECT OR UNFITNESS OF THE EQUIPMENT SHALL RELIEVE LESSEE OF THE OBLIGATION TO PAY RENT, OR ANY OTHER OBLIGATION UNDER THIS AGREEMENT OR ITS ASSIGNEE.

1. LEASE: Lessor hereby leases to Lessee and Lessee hereby hires and takes from Lessor the personal property described above and on any attached supplemental "schedule A" (hereinafter, with all replacement parts, additions, repairs, and accessories incorporated therein and/or affixed thereto, referred to as "Equipment").

2. TERM AND RENT: This Lease is non-cancelable for the term stated above and shall commence upon the Date of Acceptance of the equipment and shall continue for the period specified as the "term" stated

above. If one or more advance rentals are payable, the total amount of such advance rentals shall be set forth in the Advance Rental Payment(s) section above and shall be due upon acceptance by the Lessor of this lease. Advance rentals, when received by Lessor, shall be applied to the first rent payment for the Equipment and the balance of the advance rental shall be applied to the final rental payment or payments for said Equipment. In no event shall any advance rent or any other rent payments be refunded to Lessee.

3. Equipment is and shall at all times remain, the property of Lessor, and Lessee shall have no right, title, or interest therein, except as herein set forth, and no right to purchase or otherwise acquire title to or ownership of any of the equipment. If Lessor supplies Lessee with labels indicating that the equipment is owned by Lessor, Lessee shall affix such labels to and keep them in a prominent place on the equipment. Lessee hereby authorizes Lessor to insert in this lease the serial numbers and other identification data of equipment when determined by Lessor. Lessor is hereby appointed by Lessee as its true and lawful attorney in respect to being hereby authorized by Lessee, at Lessee's expense, to cause this lease, or any statement or other instrument in respect of this lease showing the interest of Lessor in the equipment, including Uniform Commercial Code Financing Statements, to be filed or recorded and refiled and re-recorded, and grants Lessor the right to execute Lessee's name thereto. Lessee agrees to execute and deliver any statement or instrument requested by Lessor for such purpose, and agrees to pay or reimburse Lessor for any searches, filings, recordings, or stamp fees or taxes arising from the filing or recording any such instrument or statement.

4. Lessee, at Lessee's own cost and expense, shall keep the equipment in good repair, condition, and working order and shall furnish all parts, mechanism, devices, and servicing required therefor and shall not materially alter the equipment without the consent of Lessor.

5. Lessee hereby assumes and shall bear the entire risk of loss for the theft, loss, damage, or destruction of the equipment, from any and every cause whatsoever. No such loss or damage shall impair any obligation of Lessee under this Agreement which shall continue in full force and effect. In the event of such loss or damage and irrespective of, but applying full credit for payment from any insurance coverage, Lessee shall, at its own cost and expense at the option of Lessor: (a) place the same in good repair, condition, and working order; or (b) replace the same with similar equipment of equal value; or (c) pay all the sums due and owing under this Agreement, computed from the date of such loss or damage, in which case this Agreement shall terminate, except for Lessee's duties under paragraph 9, as of the date such payment is received by Lessor.

6. Lessor shall have no tort liability to Lessee related to the equipment, and Lessee shall indemnify, defend, and hold Lessor harmless against any liabilities, claims, actions, and expenses, including court costs and legal expenses incurred by or asserted against Lessor in any way relating to the manufacture, purchase, ownership, delivery, lease, possession, use, operation, condition, return, or other disposition of the equipment by Lessor or Lessee or otherwise related to this lease, including any claim alleging latent or other defect under the doctrine of strict liability or otherwise; any other claim under the doctrine of strict liability; and any claim for patent, trademark, service mark, or copyright infringement. Each party shall give the other notice of any event covered hereby promptly following learning thereof.

7. Lessee shall keep the equipment insured against all risks of loss or damage from every cause whatsoever. Lessee shall maintain (a) actual cash value all risk insurance on the equipment, naming Lessor as <u>LOSS PAYEE</u> and (b) single limit public liability and property damage insurance of not less than $300,000 per occurrence, or such greater or lesser amount as Lessor may from time to time request on notice to Lessee, naming Lessee as Named Insured and Lessor as <u>ADDITIONAL INSURED</u> and Lessee shall be liable for all deductible portions of all required insurance. All said insurance shall be in form and amount and with companies satisfactory to Lessor. All insurance for loss or damage shall provide that losses, if any, shall be payable to Lessor, and all such liability insurance shall be in the joint names of Lessor and Lessee. Lessee shall pay the premiums therefor and deliver to Lessor the policies of insurance or duplicates thereof, or other evidence satisfactory to Lessor of such insurance coverage. Each insurer shall agree, by endorsement upon the policy or policies issued by it or by independent instrument furnished to Lessor, that it will give Lessor <u>10 DAYS</u> written notice prior to the effective date of any alteration or cancellation of such policy. The proceeds of such insurance payable as a result of loss of or damage to the equipment shall be applied at the option of Lessor, as set out in paragraph 6. Lessee hereby irrevocably appoints Lessor as Lessee's attorney-in-fact to make claim for, receive payment of, and execute and endorse all documents, checks, or drafts received in payment for loss or damage under any said insurance policies. In case of the failure of Lessee to procure or maintain said insurance or to comply with any other provision of this Agreement, Lessor shall have the right but shall not be obligated, to effect such insurance or compliance on behalf of Lessee. In that event, all money spent by and expenses of Lessor shall have the right but shall not be obligated, to effect such insurance or compliance on behalf of Lessee. In that event, all money spent by and expenses of Lessor in effecting such insurance or compliance shall be deemed to be additional rent, and shall be paid by Lessee to Lessor with the next monthly payment of rent.

8. Lessee shall pay directly, or to Lessor, all license fees, registration fees, assessments, and taxes which may now or hereafter be imposed upon the ownership, sale (if authorized), possession, or use of the equipment, excepting only those based on Lessor's income, and shall keep the equipment free and clear of all levies, liens, or encumbrances arising therefrom. Lessee shall make all filings as to and pay when due all property taxes on the equipment, on behalf of Lessor, with all appropriate governmental agencies, except where Lessor is notified by the taxing jurisdiction that Lessor must pay the tax direct, and within not more than 60 days after the due date of such filing to send Lessor a confirmation of such filing. If Lessee fails to pay any said fees, assessments, or taxes, Lessor shall have the right, but not the obligation, to pay the same and such amount, including penalties and costs, which shall be repayable to Lessor with the next installment of rent and if not so paid shall be the same as failure to pay any installment of rent due hereunder. Lessor shall not be responsible for contesting any valuation of or tax imposed on the equipment, but may do so strictly as an accommodation to Lessee and shall not be liable or accountable to Lessee therefor.

9. Time is of the essence in this agreement and no waiver by Lessor of any breach or default shall constitute a wavier of any additional or subsequent breach or default by Lessor nor shall it be a wavier of any of Lessor's rights. If any rental payment shall be unpaid for more than TEN (10) DAYS after the due date thereof. Lessor shall have the right to add and collect a reasonable late charge of five percent (5%) or a lesser amount if established by any state or federal statute applicable thereto, plus interest at the maximum rate permitted by law together with any other expense necessarily incurred by reason of such non-payment and Lessor may exercise any one or more of the remedies set forth in paragraph 12.

10. An event of default shall occur if: (a) Lessee fails to pay when due any installment of rent; (b) Lessee shall fail to perform or observe any covenant, condition, or agreement to be performed or observed by it hereunder; (c) Lessee ceases doing business as a going concern, makes an assignment for the benefit of creditors, admits in writing its inability to pay its debts as they become due, files a voluntary petition in bankruptcy, is adjudicated a bankrupt or an insolvent, files a petition seeking for itself any reorganization, arrangement, composition readjustment, liquidation, dissolution, or similar arrangement under any present or future statute, law, or regulation or files an answer admitting the material allegations of a petition filed against it in any such proceeding, consents to or acquiesces in the appointment of a trustee, receiver, or liquidator of it or all or any substantial part of its assets or properties, or if it or its shareholders shall take any action looking to its dissolution or liquidation; (d) within 60 days after the appointment without Lessee's consent or acquiescence of any trustee, receiver, or liquidator of it or of all or any substantial part of its assets and properties, such appointment

shall not be vacated, or (e) Lessee attempts to remove, sell, transfer, encumber, part with possession, or sublet the equipment or any item thereof.

11. Upon Lessee's default, the rights and duties of the parties shall be as set forth in this paragraph: (a) Acceleration: Lessor may revoke Lessee's privilege of paying the total rent installments and, upon Lessor's demand, the portion of the total rent then remaining unpaid plus all other sums due and unpaid shall promptly be paid to Lessor. (b) Retaking: at Lessor's option, Lessor may demand and Lessee must promptly deliver the equipment to Lessor. If Lessee does not so deliver, Lessee shall make the equipment available for retaking and authorizes Lessor, its employees, and nominees to enter the premises of the Lessee and other premises (insofar as Lessee can permit) for the purpose of retaking. Lessor shall not be obligated to give notice or to obtain legal process for retaking. In the event of retaking, Lessee expressly waives all rights to possession and all claims of injuries suffered through or loss caused by retaking. (c) Disposition: Lessor may sell or release the equipment and Lessee agrees to pay any deficiency resulting from the sale or releasing of the equipment. To the extent of Lessee's liability, all proceeds of the sale or releasing, or both, less all expenses incurred in retaking the goods, all expenses incurred in the enforcement of this lease, all damages that Lessor shall have sustained by reason of Lessee's default, including those incurred by obtaining a deficiency judgment and a reasonable attorney fee, shall be credited to Lessee as and when received by Lessor. Sums in excess of Lessee's liability shall belong to Lessor. (d) Unpaid Rent: The provisions of this paragraph shall not prejudice Lessor's right to recover or prove damages for unpaid rent accrued prior to default. Lessor may seek to enforce the terms of this Agreement through any court of competent jurisdiction and Lessor may seek relief other than as specified in this Agreement to the extent such relief is not inconsistent with the terms of this Agreement. Lessee agrees to pay reasonable attorney's fees and court costs incurred by Lessor in the enforcement of the terms of this Agreement. In any instance where Lessee and Lessor have entered into more than one contract, Lessee's default under any one contract shall be a default under all contracts and Lessor shall be entitled to enforce appropriate remedies for Lessee's default under each such contract.

12. Lessee shall not sell, assign, sublet, pledge, mortgage, or otherwise encumber or suffer a lien upon or against any interest in this agreement or the equipment or remove the equipment from the place of installation set forth herein, unless Lessee obtains the written consent of Lessor which consent shall not be unreasonably withheld. Lessee's interest herein is not assignable or transferable by operation of the law. Lessee agrees not to waive its right to use and possess the equipment in favor of any party other than Lessor and further agrees not to abandon the equipment to any party other than Lessor. Lessor may inspect the equipment

during normal business hours and enter the premises where the equipment may be located for such purpose. Lessee shall comply with all laws, regulations, and orders relating to this Agreement and the use, operation, or maintenance of the equipment.

13. All rights of Lessor hereunder and to the equipment may be assigned, pledged, or otherwise disposed of, in whole or in part, without notice to Lessee, but subject to the rights of Lessee hereunder. Lessee shall acknowledge receipt of any notice of assignment in writing and shall thereafter pay any amounts designated in such notice as directed therein. If Lessor assigns this lease or any interest herein, no default by Lessor hereunder or under any other agreement between Lessor and Lessee shall excuse performance by Lessee of any provision hereof. In the event of such default by Lessor, Lessee shall pursue any rights on account thereof solely against Lessor and shall pay the full amount of the assigned rental payments to the assignee. No such assignee shall be obligated to perform any duty, covenant, or condition required to be performed by Lessor under the terms of this lease.

14. This Agreement cannot be canceled or terminated by Lessee on or after the date the equipment is delivered to and accepted by Lessee. If Lessee cancels or terminates this Agreement prior to delivery or acceptance of the equipment, Lessee shall pay to Lessor (a) the value (at cost) of all equipment ordered or purchased by Lessor prior to Lessee's termination or cancellation, (b) all of Lessor's out-of-pocket expenses, and (c) a sum equal to 1% of the total rents for the lease term as liquidated damages, the exact sum of which would be extremely difficult to determine, to reasonably compensate Lessor for credit review, document preparation, ordering equipment, and other administrative expenses.

15. Upon expiration of the lease term, Lessee will immediately return the equipment in as good a condition as received, less normal wear, tear, and depreciation, to Lessor's branch office which is nearest to the place of installation or to such other reasonable place as is designated by Lessor. The equipment shall be carefully crated, shipped freight prepaid, and properly insured. Should Lessee not return the equipment at the end of the lease term, Lessee shall continue to pay rent to Lessor in the sum and on the due dates set out in this Agreement as a month-to-month lease term until returned by Lessee or demand therefor is made by Lessor.

16. This Lease Agreement consisting of the foregoing and the reverse side hereof, correctly sets forth the entire agreement between Lessor and Lessee. No agreements or understandings shall be binding on either of the parties hereto unless set forth in writing signed by the parties. The term "Lessee" as used herein shall mean and include any and all Lessees who sign hereunder, each of whom shall be jointly and severally bound thereby. No representations, warranties, or promises, guarantees, or

agreements, oral or written, express or implied, have been made by either party hereto with respect to this lease or the equipment other than set forth herein. No agent or employee of the supplier is authorized to bind Lessor to this or to waive or alter any terms or conditions printed herein or add any provision hereto. This Lease Agreement is binding upon the legal representatives and successors in interest of the Lessee. Lessee shall provide Lessor with such interim or annual financial statements as Lessor may reasonably request. In addition, Lessee warrants that the application, statements, and financial reports submitted by it to the Lessor are material inducements to the granting of this lease and that any material misrepresentations shall constitute a default hereunder. If any portion of this contract is deemed invalid, it shall not affect the balance of this Agreement.

DELIVERY AND ACCEPTANCE NOTICE

The undersigned Lessee hereby acknowledges receipt of the equipment described below or on any attached schedule (the "Equipment") fully installed and in good working condition, and Lessee hereby accepts the Equipment after full inspection thereof as satisfactory for all purposes of the above-referenced lease executed by Lessee with the Lessor. Lessee certifies that Lessor has fully and satisfactorily performed all covenants and conditions to be performed by Lessor under the Lease and has delivered the Equipment selected solely by Lessee in accordance with Lessee's directions.

LESSEE AGREES THAT THE LESSOR HAS MADE AND MAKES NO REPRE-SENTATIONS OR WARRANTIES OF ANY KIND OR NATURE, DIRECTLY OR INDIRECTLY, EXPRESS OR IMPLIED, AS TO ANY MATTER WHATSOEVER, INCLUDING THE SUITABILITY OF SUCH EQUIPMENT, ITS DURABILITY, ITS FITNESS FOR ANY PARTICULAR PURPOSE, ITS MERCHANTABILITY, ITS CONDITION, AND/OR ITS QUALITY, AND AS BETWEEN LESSEE AND LESSOR OR LESSOR'S ASSIGNEE, LESSEE LEASES THE EQUIPMENT "AS IS" AND LESSEE AFFIRMS THAT IT HAS NO DEFENSES OR COUNTECLAIMS AGAINST LESSOR IN CONNECTION WITH THE LEASE.

_____

(Lessee)

Date Equipment Accepted: _____   By: _____

20A.13   SUMMARY.   Leasing over the past several decades has become a very complicated topic, one that affects the budgetary process in a multitude of ways. The Financial Accounting Standards Board has specified the treatment of leases on balance sheets, income statements, and cash flow statements. Additionally, internal analysis, such as lease versus purchase, pushes the treatment of leasing well beyond GAAP considerations. In today's international financial milieu, the managerial expert must cross the financial Rubicon and extend the frontiers of leasing, budgeting, and finance well into heretofore uncharted domains.

SOURCES AND SUGGESTED REFERENCES

Allison, "New Rules Increase Exposure of Lessors to Tax on Rents that Will Not Be Received Until Later," *Journal of Taxation,* Vol. 64, at 8 (1986).

Amembal, Halladay, and Isom, *The Handbook of Equipment Leasing*, Publishers Press, 1988.

Amembal and Halladay, *A Guide to Accounting for Leases*, Publishers Press, 1992.

Auerback, "A Transactional Approach to Lease Analysis," 13 *Hofstra Law Review* 309 (1985).

Carson, Roger L., "Leasing, Asset Lives and Uncertainty: A Practitioner's Comments," *Financial Management*, Summer 1987.

Carter and Wight, "New Tax Law Makes Major Changes to the Foreign Tax Credit Limitation," *Journal of Taxation*, Vol. 66 at 140 (1987).

Delessio and Shenkman, "Improvement to Leased Property: Maximizing the Tax Benefits Regardless of Who Makes Them," *Taxation for Accountants*, Vol. 33, at 256 (1984).

Financial Accounting Standards Board, *Financial Accounting Standards Board Statement No. 13*, "Accounting for Leases" (November 1976).

Knight, Ray, and Lee G. Knight, "True Leases Versus Disguised Installment and Sales/Purchases," *The Tax Adviser*, March 1987.

Naughton, "International Leverage and Facility Leasing in the United States," *NYU Institute of Federal Taxation*, Vol. 44, ch. 47 (1986).

Rosen, Howard, *Leasing Law in the European Community*, Euromoney Books, 1991.

Shulman and Cox, *Leasing for Profit*, AMA, 1987.

Weisner and Massoglia, "Sec. 467 Rental Agreements: Lessors and Lessees Must Watch Their Step," *Tax Advisor*, Vol. 16 at 392 (1985).

CHAPTER 26

BUDGET BRACKETING

Michael W. Curran

Decision Sciences Corporation

CONTENTS

26.4 DEVELOPING A TACTICAL BUDGETING MODEL

(e)   Tracking and Feedback Mechanism

Page 26 • 20, replace Exhibit 26.15 with:

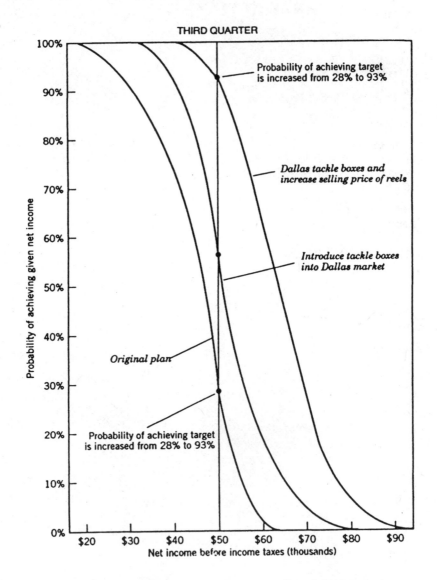

Exhibit 26.15   Fishing Supplies Company—income profiles of third quarter.

26.6 CONSOLIDATING INCOME STATEMENTS

Page 26 • 23, replace Exhibit 26.17 with:

ANNUAL EARNINGS PER SHARE			PROBABILITY OF ACHIEVING TARGET
LOWEST $1.10	TARGET $1.27	HIGHEST $1.45	72%

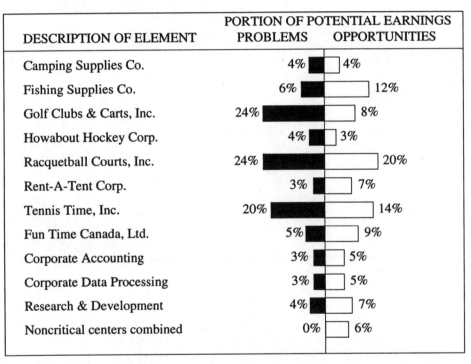

DESCRIPTION OF ELEMENT	PORTION OF POTENTIAL EARNINGS	
	PROBLEMS	OPPORTUNITIES
Camping Supplies Co.	4%	4%
Fishing Supplies Co.	6%	12%
Golf Clubs & Carts, Inc.	24%	8%
Howabout Hockey Corp.	4%	3%
Racquetball Courts, Inc.	24%	20%
Rent-A-Tent Corp.	3%	7%
Tennis Time, Inc.	20%	14%
Fun Time Canada, Ltd.	5%	9%
Corporate Accounting	3%	5%
Corporate Data Processing	3%	5%
Research & Development	4%	7%
Noncritical centers combined	0%	6%

Exhibit 26.17.   The Fun Time Company—results of computer simulation of next fiscal year..

CHAPTER **27A**

ACTIVITY-BASED BUDGETING (New)

James A. Brimson

ABM Institute

John J. Antos

Antos Enterprises, Inc.

CONTENTS

* This material has been adapted from *Activity-Based Management for Service Industries, Government Entities, and Not-for-Profit Organizations* by James A. Brimson and John J. Antos, NY, (John Wiley & Sons, Inc. 1994).

27A.1   INTRODUCTION.   The purposes of this chapter are to:

- Discuss problems with traditional budgeting
- Define activity-based budgeting (ABB)
- Discuss the ABB process.

A budget is a financial expression of a plan. Traditional budgeting focuses on planning resources for an organizational unit. Each year managers look at history and any significant changes and create an annual budget. The budgeting process starts with the senior executive announcing budget goals. These may consist of revenue and profit goals as well as goals for new services.

Many managers respond by looking at last year's numbers and increasing their budget for the year based on inflation and/or the amount of the increase in revenues (see Exhibit 27A.1). For example, if revenues increase 10%, then the various department managers might increase the budgets for their departments by 10%.

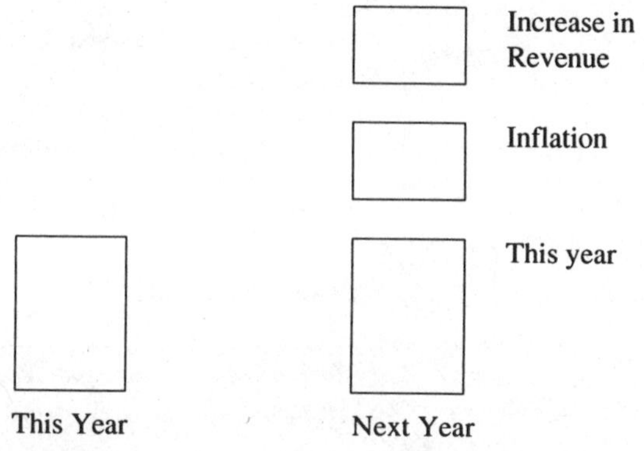

Exhibit 27A.1.   Manager's response to next year's forecast.

The problem with this approach is that last year's inefficiencies are incorporated into this year's budget. Often little attention is paid to improvements in each department. Finally, little incentive is incorporated into the budgeting process for continuous improvement. Changing workload for each department often is not considered.

Senior managers, during budgeting, often make arbitrary cuts across the board. A potentially negative consequence is that the better-managed departments may have already cut the majority of waste and now may have to cut into necessary resources. Instead, other, less-efficient departments should make more radical reductions to bring them to the same level of efficiency as the better-managed departments.

Budgets in this environment often become wrestling matches in which those who are the best presenters are given larger budgets. The theory goes that the best at presenting the reasons for the larger budget deserves the larger budget.

Once the budget is agreed on, it is often cast in concrete for the year.

27A.2   TRADITIONAL BUDGETING DOES NOT SUPPORT EXCELLENCE.   First, the budgeting process should highlight cost reduction and the elimination of wasteful activities and tasks. Traditional budgeting does not make visible what the organization does. Instead, managers look at their history of spending and simply increase last year's budget and/or actuals based on inflation and/or increases in revenue.

Second, budgeting should be a formal mechanism for reducing workload to the minimal level to support enterprise objectives. Excess workload due to poor structuring of activities and business process drives up cost and does not improve customer satisfaction. The budgeting process itself should give insight into how to reduce workload and how to set workload reduction goals.

Third, budgeting should consider all costs as variable; yet budgeting often formalizes the laissez-faire attitude toward occupancy and equipment costs. Most are familiar with the concept of fixed and variable costs. The problem with this classification is a psychological one. The term *fixed costs* seems to imply that these costs cannot be eliminated because they are fixed. Yet we all know that buildings and equipment can be put to alternative use, sold, demolished, or leased. Many assets are often dedicated to specific activities. By making these assets more flexible, the total capital base of an enterprise can be lowered. Even property taxes and property insurance can be reduced. A budget based on variable and fixed costs often focuses attention on the variable costs and implies that the fixed costs are not controllable.

A better classification would be utilized and unutilized capacity. This classification simply shows that some assets are being used and some are not. It does not present the psychological barrier to change that the term *fixed costs* does. Unutilized capacity can be saved for future growth, eliminated, used for other purposes, or consolidated with another division.

An important goal of budgeting should be to improve each process on a continuous basis. Traditional budgeting, as it is commonly practiced, seems to focus on simply repeating history. Activity budgeting sets improvement targets by activity/business process. Thus, this approach is something everyone can understand and use to work toward improvement. However, traditional budgeting sets goals like "reduce costs" by a specific percentage, without giving employees insights on how to achieve those targets.

Activity budgeting works to synchronize activities and thus improve business processes. Traditional budgeting may take the approach of "every department for itself." Managers pay lip service to coordinating between departments; however, managers will almost certainly respond in a way that will maximize their own department's performance. The inevitable consequence is to lower the performance of the organization as a whole.

Activity budgeting sets business process improvement goals, which requires the joint efforts of employees from a variety of departments. Because the goal is to improve the business process, old barriers between departments begin to crumble.

Traditional budgeting does not formally consider external and internal suppliers and customers. However, activity budgeting requires asking the internal and external suppliers and customers to describe their needs and their respective workload requirements.

Too often, the focus in traditional budgeting is to control the result. For example, consider the organization that closes its financial books in 4 to 15 days. Each month managers focus on information that is 34 to 45 days old.

It makes more sense to control the *process*, rather than to try to control the *result* through financial statements. The Japanese have unsophisticated accounting systems compared to U.S. companies of a similar size. If the secret was a more sophisticated accounting system, then U.S. companies should be superior. Yet that is not necessarily the case.

Activity budgeting and activity management focus on controlling the process. Only by controlling the process can results improve.

In a similar vein, traditional budgeting tends to focus on the effects rather than the causes. For example, it often requires a long time to hire new employees or introduce a new service. In reality, organizations should focus on the causes of these long lead times. In Japan, managers come to meetings asking their peers for suggestions to solve their problems. In the United States, our individualistic attitudes often makes managers consider a request for help as a sign of weakness. So managers make up excuses to explain the reasons they were over budget, rather than concentrating their efforts on how to improve operations.

Because activity budgeting focuses on the root cause of problems, everyone can work to identify how to reduce or eliminate them. Only by eliminating the "root cause" of the problem can the cost be permanently eliminated.

Activity budgeting requires that customers be asked for their requirements. Only by asking the customer can an organization understand whether it has properly applied resources to meet the customer's needs (e.g., do the patrons of the U.S. Postal Service want two- to three-day delivery, or do they want consistent delivery within some stated time period?). By asking the customer, the workload connected with the activities necessary to please the customer can better be determined.

Activity budgeting focuses on output, not on input. It focuses on what work is done, how the work is performed, and how much work is done. The required resources are only a consequence of the activities. The problem with traditional budgeting is that it lacks ownership. Even if the department manager "owns" the budget, seldom do the individual employees in that department own the budget. Activity budgeting asks each person to look at the activities he or she performs and set performance targets for those activities in the context of customer requirements and organizational objectives.

Activity budgeting allows people to be empowered to manage their activities properly. If something is wrong, if there is a better way to perform the activity or business process, or if a quality issue arises, the employee(s) who performs the activity or business process should make the necessary improvements or corrections without requiring management approval. (This assumes that the employee is not changing the service or the quality provided to the customer, and is improving the service or business process at a lower cost.)

Senior management needs to remember that people will not work themselves out of a job. People will contribute ideas to improve operations only if they understand that improvement in value-added activities allows the transfer of resources to growth-enabling activities.

Under activity budgeting, mistakes are acceptable, but repetition of mistakes is unacceptable. An executive told Sam Walton of a $10 million mistake and submitted his resignation. Walton told the executive he couldn't resign because the company had just spent $10 million training him. People need to know they can make mistakes, but they must learn from those mistakes and not repeat them.

Activity budgeting uses a common language—the language of the activities or business processes that everyone is performing. Traditional budgeting uses terms that the accountants are familiar with. This Tower of Babel makes communication more difficult and encourages specialization at the expense of cooperation.

Activity budgeting looks for consistency of the output. This means that the activity should be performed in a consistent way over time. Continuous improvement must be encouraged, but the activity should only be performed in accordance with current best practice. Success depends on finding the best possible way to perform an activity or business process and consistently looking for ways to improve it, while performing the activity/business process in a consistent manner.

Activity budgeting requires setting activity or business process targets as the minimum level of performance rather than the absolute level. These activity or business process targets should identify the minimum level of performance necessary to support organizational objectives. Managers should not try to exceed these minimum levels. Instead, they should look at ways to reduce waste and non-value-added portions of various activities.

27A.3   ACTIVITY-BASED BUDGETING DEFINITIONS.   Activity-based budgeting (ABB) is the process of planning and controlling the expected activities of the organization to derive a cost-effective budget that meets forecast workload and agreed strategic goals.

An **ABB** is a quantitative expression of the expected activities of the organization, reflecting management forecast of workload and financial and nonfinancial requirements to meet agreed strategic goals and planned changes to improve performance.

The three key elements of an ABB include:

- Type of work to be done
- Quantity of work to be done
- Cost of work to be done.

(a)   Principles of ABB.   ABB must reflect what is done, that is, the activities or business processes, not cost elements. Resources required (cost elements) must be derived from the expected activities or business processes and workload. *Workload* is simply the number of units of an activity that are required. For example, in the human resource department, the workload for the activity "hire employees" might be to hire 25 employees. The cost elements to perform that activity might be the wages and benefits of the recruiter, travel, advertising, testing, supplies, and occupancy costs for the space occupied by the recruiter and for interviewing. If a hiring freeze occurs, then the workload for this activity would be zero.

Budgets must be based on the future workload in order to meet:

- Customer requirements
- Organizational/departmental goals and strategies
- New/changed services and service mix
- Changes in business processes
- Improvements in efficiency and effectiveness
- Quality, flexibility, and cycle time goals
- Changes in service levels.

The final budget must reflect the changes in resource cost levels and foreign exchange fluctuations. However, it is better to initially budget using constant cost and foreign exchange rates to facilitate comparisons, and then to add inflation and foreign exchange adjustments at the conclusion of the budgeting process.

As part of the activity budgeting process, it is important to highlight continuous improvement. Each department should identify the activities or business processes to be improved, the amount of improvement, and how it plans to achieve its improvement targets.

(b)   Requirements for Successful ABB Budgeting.   The organization must be committed to excellence. If the organization does not have this commitment, then resources will be wasted on data analysis activities that will never be implemented. Changing is not easy. It is easier to study the problem than to make the difficult decisions required to improve.

(c)   Process Management Approach.   The organization must use a process management approach to improvement. This requires defining each activity as part of a repeatable, robust business process that can be continuously improved and the variability removed. Activities defined this way can use various techniques to decrease time, improve quality, and reduce the cost of those activities.

Process management is crucial to excellence, because high levels of performance are possible only when activities are done to best practices, the unused capacity is minimal, the best practices are continually made better, and the activities are executed perfectly. Activity definitions must support process management. Activities must be in the form of verb plus a noun. There must be a physical output. Two-stage definitions of drivers are usually not adequate. For example, the activity "pay employee" is compatible with process management. To define an activity as "supplies handling" and the output measure as the "number of service production runs" would not be compatible activity definitions. Two-stage activity definitions might be used in assigning costs to a service, but it does not help in improving operations. A better way to define this sample activity would be "move supplies," with the output measure defined as the "number of moves."

One of the first steps that an activity manager may have to take is to review activity definitions to make sure that they are compatible with a process approach.

(d)   Culture Encourages Sustaining Benefits.   The organization culture should encourage sustaining benefits. These benefits should not be something that lasts for only a short while, after which everyone goes back to the old way. These benefits should change the way the people in the organization think and act. Often this means changing the way the employees are compensated, so that they share in the productivity improvement.

Organizations must overcome the cultural barriers shown in Exhibit 27A.2. Next to these barriers are actions the organization must take in order to overcome these cultural barriers.

Cultural barriers	Actions
Departmental structure often interferes with departments interacting, in order to minimize total enterprise cost.	Change information systems so the organization can see total cost of business processes rather than just the costs in a specific department.
Policies and procedures provide guidelines for employee behavior. These were often set up to ensure consistency and to make it easy for employees to handle specific situations.	Empower employees to handle various situations to ensure customer satisfaction. Use policies to set general guidelines and train, support, and empower employees to satisfy the customer.
Suggestion programs usually require the approval of management to implement change. This slows the change process.	Suggestion programs are only for changes to the service or for capital requests. Changes to efficiency should be made by employees without management approval.
Measurement systems tend to focus on the department level.	Abolish micromanagement. Give managers/employees the tools, authority, and responsibility to do their jobs. Make them responsible for outputs and a budget level of resources to do their work.
Specialization assumes that lowest cost is achievable through economies of scale.	Today flexibility is critical. People must be cross-trained for a variety of tasks. First, as slack or heavy periods occur, employees can help out in other departments. Second, they need to understand how what they do affects other departments and how what other departments do affects them.

Exhibit 27A.2.   Cultural barriers.

(e)   Commitment to Excellence.   Many organizations take a short-term approach to improving operations. Costs are easy to control—simply stop spending money. This approach is similar to a crash diet. The problem with crash diets is that the dieter usually regains what he or she lost and often gains even more weight. If an organization is committed to excellence, then its goal is to change the way it does business. This is similar to changing eating habits. For example, organizations must start compensating people based on business process performance rather than the traditional actual versus budget of cost elements that most organizations have historically used.

27A.4   ACTIVITY-BASED BUDGETING PROCESS.   The activity-based budgeting process begins with the customer. The organization must determine who the customer is and what the customer wants. It must look to its competitors. Competition consists of both direct competitors and alternate services that might compete with the organization's services.

Then the organization must develop a strategy to meet customer needs. A restaurant must decide whether to be a five-star restaurant, with crystal and linen tablecloths, or to provide good food in a clean environment with less sophisticated decor but with good value to the customer.

Next, the organization should forecast workload. Management and sales determine what sales levels will be, and managers need to estimate their workloads as a result of these sales levels. Often the sales forecast includes new services and new markets, as well as any changes in strategy.

Planning guidelines must be articulated to each manager to establish the specific activity-level targets within a business process context. Eventually, every activity manager should have targets for improving his or her respective value-added activities and eliminating non-value-added activities.

Next, interdepartmental projects should be identified. Because these projects will affect the workload, as well as the activities in several departments, they must be coordinated and done prior to each manager improving his or her own activities.

At this point in the budgeting process, specific activity-level projects can be identified. These are projects to improve operations at the individual activity level. However, improvement should always be within organizational objectives, a business process context, and a customer satisfaction context.

Activity-based investment analysis consists of defining improvement projects, evaluating those projects, and then using committees to select projects that will meet the organization's goals and meet customers' needs.

The final step is to determine the activities and workload for the coming year.

27A.5   LINKING STRATEGY AND BUDGETING.   One of the problems with traditional budgeting is that a clear link between the enterprise's strategy and budgeting often does not exist. Therefore, operating managers do not know how to incorporate strategy into their budgets.

(a)   Principles of Strategic Management.   There are a variety of seminars and books available on the subject of strategic management. This chapter does not discuss those techniques, but simply assumes that a strategic plan exists. The role of senior management is to set performance targets based on the strategic plans. The performance targets might be for sales, number of new services and/or markets, cycle time, cost, quality, or customer service levels. The role of the activity manager is to achieve or exceed those targets.

Strategic objectives and performance targets must be translated into activity-level targets. Activity managers must ensure that service requirements are a direct derivative of customer needs.

The translation process starts with customer requirements and an analysis of competitive strategies. Then strategic objectives are set. The price for services allowable by the market are determined and time, quality, and cost targets are determined. Then these targets are translated into activity-level targets.

There are several important strategic management tools to assist with this process. The key ones include:

- Customer surveys
- Core competency analysis
- Benchmarking
- Quality function deployment
- Reverse engineering.

(b) Customer Surveys.   One of the first steps in the strategic management process is to perform a customer survey. The customer survey can be done in person, by telephone, or by direct mail. The survey asks a variety of questions, but the focus is on the factors that are important to the customer, a ranking of those factors by the customer, and, finally, the customer's perception of the organization's performance regarding those factors.

Based on this survey, the organization needs to start with the factors most important to the customer and determine whether it is satisfying the customer on those factors of performance. Activity or business process and investment preference must be given to those activities or business processes that the customer feels are most important. Especially in the case where satisfaction levels are not satisfactory to the customer, the organization needs to change, improve, or increase resources and effectiveness of those activities or business processes.

For example, if an organization determines that it needs to allow nurses to spend more time with patients and less time doing paperwork, then it could create an activity budget in the following way:
For the activity "complete medical charts":

Total cost	Salaries	Depreciation	Supplies	Phone	Occupancy
$24,410	22,000	400	900	150	960

The assumptions are that a person would be hired to "complete medical charts." The employee's salary and benefits would be $22,000 per year. Depreciation on his or her desk and computer would be $400. Supplies connected with filling out the charts are estimated to be $900. Because this person would be communicating with other departments, a phone would be necessary for inter-hospital calls. The fully loaded cost of hospital space (including depreciation, heat, electricity, building maintenance, and janitorial cost based on the number of square feet occupied) equals $960.

Hiring this person will enable 10 nurses to spend 10% of their time comforting, informing, and answering questions for patients. A nurse earns $36,000 annually, including benefits.

For the activity "communicate with patients":

Total cost	Salaries	Depreciation	Supplies	Phone	Occupancy
$46,320	36,000	1,000	2,000	320	7,000

The following assumptions were made. Annual salaries and benefits for 10 nurses at $36,000 per nurse equals $360,000. Because they will spend 10% of their time on this activity, the salary portion of this activity cost equals $36,000. There would be some depreciation on the desk for the portion of time performing this activity. Some educational literature would be given to the patients, which would total approximately $2,000. Nurses would need a phone line for tracking down answers to patient questions, and a reasonable percentage of the total phone cost was estimated at $320. Because the nurses spent some time sitting at a desk for this activity, 10% of their total occupancy costs was apportioned, which amounted to $7,000.

Now senior management can look at the customer survey and performance as it relates to nurses communicating and comforting patients—a high-priority item in the eyes of the customer. Then they can determine if it is worth spending a total of $70,730 ($24,410 plus $46,320) to improve customer satisfaction in this area.

(c)   Core Competency Analysis.   An organization starts by asking what activities or business processes are critical to its industry. These activities or business processes become the *core competencies* of that industry. Then the organizations can ask themselves which activities or business processes they perform well. They need to compare themselves with external benchmarks and determine where there is a core competency gap. Then the organizations can set budget targets in terms of cost, quality, and time.

Industry	Core competency
Banking	Accuracy, fast turnaround, full service
Insurance	Low rates, knowledgeable representatives, fast claims handling
Hospitals	Friendly nurses, full service, high success rate
Airlines	On-time, convenient departures, reasonable fares
Fast food	Quality, service, cleanliness
IRS	Rules that are easy to comply with, fairness, easy access
Fund-raisers	Good cause, large percentage of funds directly to cause

An auto dealer decided that a core competency of the repair shop was to provide quality repairs the first time. A further analysis revealed an opportunity to improve performance by conducting auto repair training seminars for the mechanics. Four seminars for 20 mechanics who earn $14 per hour were planned. Each seminar was to be five hours long with $500 in training supplies. A consultant will charge $3,000 per training session.

For the activity "train mechanics":

Total cost	Salaries	Supplies	Phone	Consultant
$18,100	5,600	500	0	12,000

(d) Benchmarking. The benchmarking process compares performance to other organizations, either internally or externally. Benchmarks may measure:

- Activities
- Business processes
- Time
- New service introduction
- Customer service
- Quality
- Cost.

Comparisons should be made, where possible, across divisions, with competitors, and with the best organizations in the world. For example, one telephone company can process a request for new phone service within 43 seconds. This is a speed few other organizations can duplicate, and would serve as a great benchmark for the activity "process new customers' credit requests."

One association felt it was important to answer the phone after only two rings. This would be a high-quality service to the members, and would avoid lost sales of books and seminars because people tired of waiting for someone to answer the phone. The association's operators were currently answering the phone on the third or fourth ring. It decided to increase the number of telephone operators by three. Telephone operators could be hired for $18,000 per year. They would need a desk, a PC, a phone, and supplies for order taking. Fully loaded occupancy costs were running $10 per square foot. Each operator would need 64 square feet of space.

For the activity "answer phones":

Total cost	Salaries	Depreciation	Supplies	Phone	Occupancy
$60,120	54,000	2,000	1,200	1,000	1,920

(e) Quality Function Deployment. Quality function deployment (QFD) is a concept originating in the quality field, and is applicable to activity budgeting. In QFD, the organization compares the customers' requirements with the activities or business processes necessary to meet those requirements. For each activity or business process, a comparison is also made with the competition to determine how the organization is doing against the competition. Also, a correlation is made between activities to show which activities have a strong positive or strong negative correlation with meeting customer requirements. Some activities will have no correlation with each other. Finally, a correlation is made between various activities and customer requirements. Thus the organization can determine which activities are critical to greatest customer satisfaction. Customer requirements are ranked as part of this analysis.

Although a complete explanation of this technique can be found in a number of quality books and seminars, a simple example will be discussed here. An airline is looking to increase market share by better satisfying its customers. Using QFD, the airline determines that quick turnaround time is important in order to have on-time departures. One way to improve in this area is to have two jetbridges to load passengers instead of only one. There are two activities—"move jetbridge" and "maintain jetbridge"—connected with this second jetbridge.

The airline determines that 10 percent of a ticketing agent's time is needed to handle this second jetbridge. A ticketing agent earns $32,000 per year. Two hundred ticketing agents will be affected. This means that salaries with benefits dedicated to the activity "move jetbridge" would be $640,000 (200 x 10% x $32,000). An additional 100 jetbridges would have to be purchased, at the rate of $10,000 per jetbridge. Therefore, the depreciation on $1,000,000 (100 x $10,000) using a five-year life would be $200,000 per year. The annual cost of maintenance labor is $100,000 on these jetbridges and is $50,000 on maintenance parts. Occupancy costs are $20,000 for the maintenance space needed for these jetbridges.

For the activities "move jetbridge" and "maintain jetbridge":

Activity	Activity cost	Salaries	Depreciation	Parts	Occupancy
Move jetbridge	640,000	640,000			
Maintain jetbridge	370,000	100,000	200,000	50,000	20,000
Total cost	1,010,000	740,000	200,000	50,000	20,000

(f)   Reverse Engineering.   Reverse engineering involves studying a competitor's services. At first glance, one would think that reverse engineering is a concept that applies only to products. However, applying reverse engineering to a service and seeing how competitors perform the service is a very useful tool.

For example, consider a company that has a regulatory affairs department that must file with the FDA to get regulatory approval. The company's managers studied the process of filing for regulatory approval. The objective was to determine how to perform the process more effectively.

Using reverse engineering principles, they started by asking the customer, in this case the FDA, the testing requirements in order to get this new product approved. Then, based on the FDA comments, they improved how they designed their products and their testing procedures in order to get approval more quickly.

For the activity, "improve the FDA approval process," the following activity costs are determined:

Regulatory personnel with salaries of $50,000 will spend 10% of their time on this project. They will have travel costs amounting to $3,000. Supplies are expected to run $600. A seminar on this topic will cost $1,700. A 10% share of their office occupancy cost is running $2,000 per year.

For the activity "improve FDA approval process":

Total cost	Salaries	Travel	Supplies	Seminar	Occupancy
$12,300	5,000	3,000	600	1,700	2,000

27A.6   TRANSLATE STRATEGY TO ACTIVITIES.   Strategy must be translated to an activity level to identify necessary changes. An example of a translating procedure follows:

Steps	Example
Define mission statement with enterprise goals	Dominate the market and diversify where advantage can be applied
Establish critical success factors	Grow market share; increase new service sales as percent of total sales
Establish service targets	Increase market share: Service 1 by 7%; Service 2 by 8%; discontinue Service 3
Establish service level targets	Service 1: increase sales 5%; decrease cost 8%; deliver in 2 hours

(a)   Identify Activity Targets by Bill of Activities.   The next step is to identify activity targets for each service.

For example: the mission might be to dominate the consumer loan business in Dallas; the critical success factor might be to grow market share; the service target might be to grow auto loan revenue by 7%; and the service level targets might be to increase auto loan sales by 5% and decrease cost by 8%.

Bill of Activities

Activity description	Cost/ output $	Units of output	Cost of service $	Target activity reduction %	$	Target cost of service $
Take application	100	1	100	<5%>	<5>	95
Order reports	50	3	150	<10%>	<15>	135
Review loans	200	1	200	<7%>	<14>	186
Complete paperwork	25	4	100	<30%>	<30>	70
Disburse funds	250	1	250			250
TOTALS			800	<8%>	<64>	736

This table shows that the employees have established cost reduction targets for four of the five activities. The total reduction of $64 is an 8% reduction from last year's bill of activity cost.

Once these strategic management tools are employed, then cost, time, and quality targets can be set by the employees for each activity. The following is an example of cost, time, and quality targets.

(b)   Strategic Management Tools and Targets.

Tool	Activity	Cost	Time	Quality
Customer survey	Communicate with patients	C: 46,320 T: 40,000	C: 10 minutes T: 30 minutes	C: 80% satisfaction T: 90%
Core competency	Train mechanics	C: 18,100 T: 22,000	C: 20 hours T: 24 hours	C: 9% redos T: 5% redos
Bench-marking	Answer phone	C: 60,120 T:	C: 4 rings T: 2 rings	C: T:
Quality function deployment	Move & maintain jetbridge	C: 1,010, 000 T: 900,000	C: 45 minutes T: 30 minutes	C: 85% T: 90% on time
Reverse engineering	Obtain FDA approval	C: 12,300 T: 10,000	C: 5 years T: 2 years	C: 75% T: 80% approval
		C = Current	T = Target	

(c)   Match Resource to Goals.   Next, match resources to goals. Goals should be set to be achievable. Resources should be oriented toward goals. Identify improvements to business processes as well as activities.

27A.7   DETERMINE WORKLOAD.   There are three major steps in determining activity or business process workload. These include:

1. Forecast service-determined activities or business processes.
2. Forecast non-service-related activities or business processes.
3. Forecast special projects.

(a)   Workload of Service-Determined Activities or Business Processes.   The first step in forecasting total organization workload is to forecast workload for service-determined activities:

- Identify activities for new services
- Identify planned changes to services
- Create/update a bill of activities for each service line
- Forecast services by service lines rather than individual services, in most cases
- Explode bill of activities to determine activity quantity for each service line.

(b)   Explode Bill of Activities.   To explode a bill of activities, simply list each service line and the forecasted quantity of that service line. List the units of each activity used by each service line. Then multiply units of service times the units of each activity to calculate the activity quantity volume by service. Then sum the total activity quantities.

Service	Units of Service	Bill of activity units required for each service	Activity quantities
Mortgages	5,000	Order report 3	15,000
Auto loans	1,800	Order report 1	1,800
Personal loans	1,000	Order report 1	1,000
		Total Reports	17,800

(c) Workload for Non-Service-Related Activities. The second step is to forecast workload of non-service-related activities. Non-service-related activities are those performed by support departments such as MIS, human resources, security, and accounting.

Activity Class	Activity Measures
General management	# of employee
Financial reporting	# of financial reports
Corporate advertising	# of TV advertisements
	# of promotions
Marketing	# of trade shows
	# of market surveys
Research	# of new services
Facilities	# of square feet

(d) Workload for Special Projects. The third step is to forecast workload for special projects. Examples of special projects include:

- Install activity-based management
- Install activity-based budgeting
- Install new computer system
- Expand office.

Then the organization needs to set up a calendar for each special project, with the activities and tasks listed by time period.

27A.8 ABB CALENDAR.

Brief senior management	*					
Select team	**					
Select departments/services		**				
Review activity definitions			****			
Review strategic plan				****		
Explode Bill of Activities					****	
Start improvement projects						***

Each * equals a week

27A.9   CREATE PLANNING GUIDELINES.   An organization should identify activity or business process-level projects with the goal of continuous improvement. Look at the budgeted workload and divide it into mandatory, discretionary, and optional units for each activity or business process. This split helps to decide what portion of value-added activities to eliminate. For example, an organization might determine that it needs only one quote to purchase supplies. The workload to obtain quotes is the minimum mandatory work. Discretionary work occurs when the purchasing agent believes a lower price is obtainable through two quotes. For optional work, the agent feels better by getting three or four quotes, some of which are from noncertified vendors.

27A.10   IDENTIFY INTERDEPARTMENTAL PROJECTS.   The organization should look at its business processes to eliminate duplicate activities and synchronize the remaining ones. Consider the following business process to "procure supplies."

(a)   Activity-Based Budget for Procuring Supplies.

Activity		Labor	Technology	Facility	Utilities	Supplies	Travel	Other	Total
LY	P	89088		7827	1293	1075	4000	162	103445
TY	Q								
LY	I	101479		8915	1472	1225	4000	175	117266
TY	P								
LY	A	108404	190299	9524	1573	1308	4000	187	315295
TY	P								
LY	S	29211		2568	424	353	5562	50	38168
TY	S								
LY	M	65545		5871	938	578	200	111	73243
TY	A								

PQ = Prepare Quotes; IP = Issue Purchase Order; AP = Administer P.O.; SS = Source supplies; MA = Manage Area; LY = Last year; TY = This Year

After reviewing last year's total costs for each activity, the next step is to calculate last year's unit cost for each activity. For example, the activity "prepare quotes" cost $103,445. Last year, 2,000 quotes were prepared. By dividing annual quotes into total cost, the unit cost for this activity is $51.72 per quote.

Activities	Workload measures	Volume	Total cost $	Unit cost $	Target cost $
Prepare quotes	Quotes	2,000	103,445	51.72	50.00
Issue P.O.	P.O.	5,679	117,265	20.65	19.65
Administer P.O.	P.O.	5,679	315,295	55.52	53.00
Source supplies	New suppliers	100	38,167	381.68	375.00
Manage area	staff	28	72,243	2,580	2,200

(b)   ABB Example of Target Cost.   The organization has set a target of $50 per quote. This is a reduction of $1.72 from last year's cost of $51.72 per quote. The improvement process for 2,000 quotes at $1.72 per quote results in a savings of $3,440. Managers feel that they can reduce supplies by $440 by keeping more information on the computer and less on paper. Travel could be reduced $1,000 by having more vendors come to the organization's offices. Because quotes will be kept on the computer, there will be a reduction in the filing activity, saving $2,000 for part-time employee wages and benefits.

(c) Creative Thinking Approaches.   Continuous improvement requires innovative approaches to streamlining the way an activity is done. Although creativity is a very personal trait, studies have shown that certain environments and methods are better suited to drawing out creative ideas. Some of the more effective methods are:

1. Challenging assumptions about:
   - people
   - supplies
   - business processes
   - location
   - capital
   - automation
   - activities.
2. Viewing activities or business processes based on new assumptions.
3. Perceiving patterns from other:
   - divisions
   - offices
   - services
   - departments.
4. Making connections with other organizations.
5. Establishing networks between suppliers, supplier's suppliers, you, customers, and end users.
6. Exploiting failures (e.g., the glue for Post-It-Notes was too weak).
7. Performing activity or business process backward and from the middle.
8. Using idea triggers (e.g., a new idea for each of Baskin & Robbins 31 flavors).
9. Creating superheroes.
10. Imagining you are the service, activity, or business process.

(d) Brainstorming.   Brainstorming techniques are fairly common today. They consist of:

1. Suspending judgment until all ideas are on the table.
2. Emphasizing quantity of ideas without worrying about quality.
3. Stimulating a freewheeling session, with wild ideas encouraged.
4. Involving people from throughout the organization.
5. Reminding people that wild ideas often will fertilize the thinking process.

(e) Storyboarding.   Storyboarding is a creativity tool that consists of using colored index cards to show business processes, activities, and tasks. The first step is to define the department mission statement. For a hotel, the department mission for the maids might be: "to keep rooms clean in order to delight customers at a minimum cost."

ACTIVITIES

	Stock cart	Clean rooms	Empty carts
T	Stack towels	Empty trash	Dispose garbage
A	Stack linens	Change bedsheets	Separate linens/towels
S	Stack toiletries	Clean bathroom	Store cart/vacuum
K	Stack stationery	Restock toiletries	
S	Stack cleaning supplies	Replace towels	
		Dust room	
		Vacuum room	
		Refill stationery	

(f) Value Management.   Value management is an organized way of thinking. It is an objective appraisal of functions performed by services and procedures. The focus is on necessary functions for the lowest cost. It increases reliability and productivity. Costs are decreased. Value management challenges everything an organization does.

It starts by gathering information such as:

- The purpose and use of each service
- The operating and performance issues
- The physical and environmental requirements.

For example, fresh fish must be kept cold. Jewelry must be kept in a secure environment. What types of support requirements are there? What problems exist? Which and how many liaison personnel are required? What are the economic issues?

These requirements are translated into required functionality of the service. Begin by determining the worth of each portion of the service. Then calculate the value improvement potential. What part of the service does the customer want? Which parts add cost? Which part is the customer willing to pay for?

Begin using creativity. Ask the customers to value different features. Ask suppliers for ideas. Use cross-functional teams and brainstorming. Use reverse engineering techniques and look at the competitor's services. Benchmark in other industries. Find the best customer service, warehousing, and order fulfillment organization. Eliminate part of the service. How can the organization create more commonality of services and support services as well as common reports and forms?

Evaluate whether it would be better to buy a portion of the service from outside (e.g., catering/training/maintenance for airlines; check processing and MIS for banks; body work for car dealers; janitorial, engineering, waste collection for cities) or to perform those services and support services in-house. Analyze customer trade-off of cost and features. Calculate value versus cost to produce various portions of the service. Eliminate functions, procedures, and reports. Simplify procedures, business processes, and functions. Use alternate supplies, specifications, and methods. Shorten the service operation cycle with cross-training of departments.

(g)   Task Level Analysis.   Sometimes it is useful to analyze the tasks of an activity in order to determine the improvement potential. For example, the activity "pay vendor invoice" has the following tasks:

Task	Total	Non-value-added	Value-added	Best practice
Receive P.O. (PO)	.50	.50		
Locate receiver (R)	.50	.50		
Get vendor invoice (I)	.50	.50		
Match PO, R, I	2.00	2.00		
Enter data	4.50		4.50	2.00
Determine errors	2.50	2.50		
Expedite payment	1.25	1.25		
Make payment: computer	3.00		3.00	2.75
Make payment: manual	1.00	1.00		
Document file	3.00	1.50	1.50	1.25
	18.75	9.75	9.00	6.00

27A.11   IMPROVEMENT PROCESS.   The improvement process starts with creative thinking to determine solutions. An investment proposal is then prepared. Management selects the projects that have the highest priority in meeting customer needs. The solution is implemented and incorporated into the activity budget.

(a)   Ranking Budget Requests.   After all the budget requests have been made, they are ranked. One convenient way to rank them is through a rating system in which management looks at the budget requests in comparison with the customer needs. Another useful tool is to classify them according to whether they support the current level of service or whether they are at the minimum or intermediate. "Current" implies that this is the cost of activities as they are presently performed. "Minimum" implies that this is the minimum level of service for an activity. "Intermediate" implies that this is not a final solution.

(b)   Impact of Projects.   Then the organization should look at the impact of these projects in terms of the change in workload, but also in terms of the changes in activity or business process cost.

27A.12   FINALIZING THE BUDGET.   Budget proposals are created for the most promising projects. They should be reviewed and the highest priority projects selected. An implementation plan should be conceived. An activity impact report should be generated to include its cost impact, assuming no inflation or foreign currency issues. This allows for comparisons with previous activity or business process performance. Finally, inflation and foreign currency should be incorporated into the budget.

(a) Budget Review Panels. Budget review panels should consist of cross-functional teams whose purpose is to question and review the budget. A review panel might consist of the directors, support departments such as human resources, administration, quality, finance, and operations.

(b) Budgeting Options. An organization has two options for activity budgeting. First, budget and report by activities. Second, budget by activities and convert the activity budget into a traditional cost element budget. In this second approach, the organization plans on an activity or business process basis. Managers would use activity costs per unit to determine cost elements. Then they would summarize by cost elements. This second approach is only temporary until the organization better understands how to manage by activities, and usually lasts for only a year.

(c) Steps in Implementing ABB.

Activities/tasks	Months			
	1	2	3	4
Train and educate	**			
Perform strategic analysis	****			
Forecast workload	******			
Establish planning guidelines	****			
Propose interdepartmental improvement		****		
Propose activity improvement			********	
Select improvement options			*******	
Finalize budget				***

Each * equals one week.

(d) Initial Project. A steering group of three to five members should be created. A series of panels with five to six members from different departments should be created to discuss cross-departmental issues. Each budgeting unit should have a budgeting manager, which could be someone other than the department manager. There would be 10 to 20 budgeting units per in-house coordinator or per consultant.

27A.13 PERFORMANCE REPORTING. Remember that the most effective reports are those that do not have to be made. Therefore, introduce proactive control rather than reactive cost monitoring wherever possible. Activity-based budgeting encourages this approach.

Emphasis should be made to control the process so that output is consistent. Also, make sure resources can be shifted when workload varies—workload seldom stays the same throughout the year. Plan and budget for using those slack times to improve the organization.

(a) Data Capture. There are three methods for data capture within an ongoing system. First, there is *dedicated resources.* Set up cost centers and define workload measures at the activity or business process level. Second, there is *shared resources,* in which an organization does time reporting by activity. Third, use a *surrogate* in which actual outputs are used at a standard activity cost. Actual costs would be compared to total department earned cost in this approach. Total actual cost could also be compared to best practices earned value.

(b)   Activity-Based Budget Report.

Department Total			Activity Analysis			
Expense	Budget $	Actual $	Issue P.O.	Certify vendor	Expedite order	Other
Wages	180,000	180,00				
Supplies	40,000	38,000				
Space	30,000	30,000				
Equipment	18,000	18,000				
Travel	22,000	20,000				
Other	10,000	8,000				
Total	200,000	194,000				
Output measure			# of P.O.	# of certification	# of orders	
Charge rate			$50	$2,000	$10	$9,000
Budgeted volume			3,000	20	100	1
Budgeted value	200,000		$150,000	$40,000	$1,000	$9,000
Actual volume			2,700	18	90	1
Earned value		181,000	$135,000	$36,000	$900	$9,100
Earned value variance		13,000				

In this example, the organization budgeted the activity "issue purchase orders" at $50 per purchase order. It budgeted 3,000 purchase orders. This yielded a budgeted value for the "issue purchase order" activity of $150,000. The same activity budgeting process was followed for the remaining activities, including an "other" or miscellaneous category of activities. This yielded a total activity budget for this department of $200,000, which was backflushed back into expense categories.

The actual expenses for the period were $194,000. Compared to the original budget of $200,000, this looks very good. However, when the earned value is calculated, the department is shown to have an earned value variance of $13,000. Earned value is calculated for each activity by multiplying the actual volume for each activity by that activity's charge rate. For the "issue purchase order" activity, the actual volume of 2,700 purchase orders when multiplied by the charge rate of $50 yields $135,000. The same calculation is made for all activities and the answers added for each department. This earned value total of $181,000 is compared to actual expenses of $194,000 to yield an earned value variance of a negative $13,000. This is a different picture than simply comparing actual with budget, which yielded a favorable variance of $6,000. Managers can now use this as a planning tool as well as a means to operate the organization more efficiently.

(c)   **Business Process Reporting.**   In business process reporting, activity cost could be shown for each department, as well as for each business process that delivers a service. This is an exercise for organizations that are more advanced in ABB techniques.

27A.14   SUMMARY.   Activity-based budgeting gives managers the tools they need to make better decisions about running their organization. This budgeting technique spends most of the time on improvement rather than filling out forms, which is often the case with traditional budgeting. This technique gives managers a method to improve activities as well as business processes.

SOURCES AND SUGGESTED REFERENCES

Antos, John J., "Activity-Based Management for Service, Not-for-Profit, and Government Organizations, " *Journal of Cost Management,* Vol. 6, No. 2, 1992.

Brimson, James A., and Antos, John J., *Activity-Based Management,* New York, John Wiley & Sons, Inc., 1994.

Brimson, James A., *Activity Accounting,* New York, John Wiley & Sons, Inc., 1991.

Brimson, James A., *Activity-Based Investment Management,* New York, American Management Association, 1989.

INDEX

Note: A page number with an "s" designation refers to a supplement page.